Start & Run a Copywriting Business

Steve Slaunwhite

Self-Counsel Press
(a division of)
International Self-Counsel Press Ltd.
USA   Canada

Self-Counsel Press acknowledges the financial support of the Government of Canada through the Book Publishing Industry Development Program (BPIDP) for our publishing activities.

Printed in Canada.

First edition: 2001

Second edition: 2005

Library and Archives Canada Cataloguing in Publication

Slaunwhite, Steve
    Start and run a copywriting business / Steve Slaunwhite. -- 2nd ed.

(Self-counsel business series)
ISBN 1-55180-633-9

1. Advertising copy. 2. New business enterprises--Planning. I. Title. II. Series.
HF5825.S56 2005   659.13'20'68   C2005-902802-5

Self-Counsel Press
(a division of)
International Self-Counsel Press Ltd.

1704 North State Street   1481 Charlotte Road
Bellingham, WA 98225   North Vancouver, BC V7J 1H1
USA   Canada

Contents

Checklists

Samples

Table

Acknowledgments

I would like to thank the many copywriters who have inspired me throughout the years — many of whom agreed to be interviewed for this book — including Ivan Levison, Donna Baier Stein, Bob Bly, Karen Levenson-Code, Steve Manning, David Garfinkel, Alan Sharpe, Dan Kennedy, Janice King, Randall Rensch, Brent Brotine, Brenda Kruse, Heather Martin, Mal Warwick, Herschell Gordon Lewis, Richard Armstrong, and Ron Marshak.

Special thanks to Richard Day for championing the book, and to Sharon Boglari whose ideas and attention to detail made this a much better manuscript than I originally submitted.

This book is for Sue.

Preface

When I wrote the first edition of this book in 2001, my goal was to create the most complete how-to guide available on the subject — packed with information to help you learn the craft, set up your office, get clients, and make money.

Since that time a lot has changed. The growth of the Internet has revolutionized the business and created a wealth of new opportunities. In addition to the dozens of top-rated copywriters I originally interviewed for this book, I've since spoken with more than one hundred — some of the most highly paid in the world — and learned their inside secrets to success.

Here's the good news: You'll find all this new information in this completely revised 2nd edition. For example:

- Updated details on setting up your copywriter's office.

- Expanded data on the markets available for your services, including insights into three of the most lucrative markets of all.

- A completely revised and expanded chapter on how to get clients — and get them fast.

- Updates on how to complete typical copywriting tasks, with the addition of e-mail marketing, websites, microsites, e-zines, and blogs.

- An expanded troubleshooting guide, based on the hundreds of letters and e-mails I've received from readers over the years.

- A bonus CD-ROM packed with resources, ready-to-use forms, and checklists — all tailored specifically to the copywriting business.

- And much, much more.

So even if you have the original edition, I encourage you to "upgrade." This *new* edition contains the latest information you need to succeed in this exciting business.

I wrote in the original preface to this book that many of us who are freelance copywriters lead a charmed life. (At least, we think so!) We spend our days happily ensconced in our comfortable home offices doing what we love to do — which is to write.

Sure, there are ups and downs: client demands, challenging projects, deadlines. They come with the territory. But most copywriters I know love the creative, stimulating work; earn high fees; and enjoy an ever-increasing demand for their services.

Do you need writing experience? It helps. But, as you'll read in the following pages, you'll be amazed how many highly successful copywriters started with little or no background in writing, marketing, or even general business. In fact, one of the most highly paid copywriters I know was, just a few years ago, a kitchen renovation contractor!

So you may be a freelance magazine writer looking for a higher-paying market … a consultant seeking a new revenue stream … a marketing or advertising professional interested in going out on your own … a stay-at-home mom or dad needing to earn some income on a flexible schedule … a corporate employee dreaming of working from home in your jammies … or even a freelance copywriter who wants to become even more successful …

Whatever your reasons for picking up this new edition, *Start & Run a Copywriting Business* may be just the opportunity you're looking for.

Interested? Read on.

1
Adventures in the Copywriting Business

Being a self-employed copywriter can be a lot of things. It can be fun, creative, challenging, invigorating, lucrative, tough, intensive, scary, relaxing, stressful, a pleasure, and a pain — but, thankfully, not all at the same time. One thing it's *not,* though, is boring. Copywriting is always an adventure.

Personally, I get a kick out of the new creative projects that hit my desk each week. One day it's an ad; the next, a website. This week, for example, I'm working on a series of brochures for an insurance company. I'm also writing an annual report for a large software firm. I enjoy learning about new products and services. And, like all writers, I love seeing my work published in the dozens of ads, brochures, websites, direct mail, and other material I write each year.

A Great Home-Based Business Opportunity

When it comes to a home-based business, copywriting is (in my opinion) as good as it gets. I can think of few pursuits that offer a more optimal mix of low risk and high income potential. Hanging your shingle requires little more than a computer, business cards and stationery, and a desk to work on. Yes, a little writing talent and marketing savvy help, but not as much as you might think. Perseverance and a willingness to learn can take you a long way (as they did for me).

As a copywriter, you can expect to be well paid. Self-employment gurus Paul and Sarah Edwards report in their book, *The Best Home-Based Businesses for the 21st Century,* that an established, self-employed copywriter can earn between $80,000 and $175,000 a year. This seems a little high to me, but most copywriters I know do earn at least $50,000 a year, with some incomes creeping well over the six-figure mark.

Freelance copywriting, I might add, can also generate a good income from working on a part-time or casual basis. Just one project per month — whether it's an ad, a brochure, or a website — can earn you an extra income of several hundred dollars per month. Many freelance copywriters I interviewed for this book began writing copy part time, slowly developing their skills, knowledge, and client base until they were ready to make a full-time commitment. I began part time, and the money I earned and lessons I learned went a long way toward more successfully launching my full-time business.

If you're a freelance writer used to the pittance magazines often pay, copywriting can greatly augment your income. This is because the magazine market is a buyer's market — with plenty of writers willing to work for free, simply to see their name in print. It's tough to break into, and even tougher to earn decent fees for your work.

Copywriters, however, encounter a demand for their services. As I explain later in this chapter, it's not exactly a seller's market, but it's close to it. And there is certainly no reason for you to accept a copywriting assignment for little or no fee. Even as a beginner, you can expect to earn good fees for the work you do.

Just how much experience and expertise do you need to earn these great fees? Obviously, the more experience you have, the greater your chance of success. But don't let a perceived lack of direct experience prevent you from tackling your goal of becoming a self-employed copywriter. Operating a successful copywriting business essentially involves a combination of writing ability and marketing strategy. If you have a modicum of the first, you can learn the second in this book.

Copywriting is a subset of business writing. Think about the business documents you've written: memos, reports, proposals, query letters. Were some of these written to persuade others to act or make a decision, or to steer them to your point of view? If so, then you already have some experience as a copywriter. Even if you haven't, your love of writing and commitment to learning the unique strategies and approaches to crafting effective marketing copy are the keys to succeeding in this business.

Copywriting is "... a broad term. The words on a menu are copy. So are the words in an ad, product description, press release, annual report, announcement, invitation, package insert, sales letter, web page, broadcast fax, CD-ROM presentation, and food label."

— *Elements of Copywriting* by Robert W. Bly and Gary Blake

What Is Copywriting?

A few of years ago, while attending a business networking event, a man introduced himself to me and asked, "What do you do?" When I explained that I'm a copywriter, he immediately launched into a long story about his nephew, a patent and trademarks lawyer. "He works with copyrights all the time," he told me. "Perhaps you know him?" I tried, of course, to explain that I don't copyright anything. I am a copy*writer*. But to no avail.

So, no, copywriting does not involve trademarks, patents, and copyright. Copywriting is a creative process of organizing information and writing words (and sometimes suggesting concepts, structure, and visuals) used in creating effective sales and marketing documents. These include print ads, Internet banner ads, brochures, case studies, direct mail, sales letters, sale sheets, flyers, case studies, and new product announcements — in fact, the list is endless.

Copywriters seek to inform, persuade, and sell. The process sometimes goes by other names — marketing writing, sales writing, persuasive writing, ad writing, and public relations writing are just a few. Sales letter guru Herschell Gordon Lewis likes to call it "force communication." Mal Warwick, an authority on fundraising letters, refers to the process simply as "writing for results."

My definition? When my wife comes home from work and asks me what I did that day, I often reply, "I wrote about segregated life insurance" or "I wrote about industrial imaging sensors." So for me, copywriting is writing persuasively about products and services and the benefits they bring to the lives of customers. Tom Stoyan, author and sales coach, teaches that selling is "influencing the thinking of others to get them emotionally involved in an idea to help them make a buying decision." Copywriting is very similar. And it's not a bad way to spend the day.

Copywriting versus Other Types of Writing

"But wait a minute," you say. "Isn't copywriting just good business writing?"

Well, yes and no.

Materials

Copywriting does have everything to do with good, clear business writing. In fact, "copy" can refer to the written text of any type of document. But the term "copywriting" is more commonly used in reference to sales, advertising, and marketing materials; effectively and persuasively writing these requires finding a unique approach to a specific, often skeptical audience.

Copywriting is a subset of business writing, which is a catch-all term encompassing a wide range of business documents and audiences. The thousands of documents written and produced by a major corporation, for example, might include any of the following:

- HTML help menus from the technical service department

- Press releases from the public relations department

- Countless e-mails, letters, memos, and reports written by executives and support staff

- Employee newsletters published by the employee communications office

- Invitations to shareholder meetings produced by investor relations

Audience

The above list of materials can be targeted at audiences as diverse as managers, CEOS, customers, employees, vendors, the media, and colleagues.

Where does copywriting fit in? You'll usually find this type of writing in the marketing department, or plied at an advertising agency or design firm. While business writing is broad, copywriting has a more specialized focus. At its most basic level, copywriting seeks to gain the attention of buyers and communicate successfully with them. Buyers may be current customers, past customers, new customers, or potential customers. Of course, the skills of persuasive writing — so deliberately applied by copywriters — can be used to great effect in many other documents (a proposal to upper management is one such example). But a copywriter's ultimate concern is how to craft headlines, sentences, and paragraphs that will tweak a buyer's interest and nudge him or her closer to making a decision to buy.

Writing that sells

Many copywriters call copywriting "writing that sells," but sometimes the direct sales message within a marketing document isn't obvious.

Direct mail certainly packs a deliberate sales punch. A direct mail package is designed to get you to make an immediate buying decision, and the success of a mailing is measured by how many people from a given list respond. But marketing documents such as case studies, success stories, and features take more of a "soft sell" approach. They contain no direct "buy now" message. Still, copywriters tasked with writing any form of marketing document, whether it be hard sell or soft sell, will use all the persuasive tools at their command in a deliberate attempt to win the hearts and minds of buyers.

Style and structure

Copywriting can also differ from general business writing in style and structure. Here's an example.

On the one hand, a technical writer trying to explain the safety procedures of a welding torch might write this:

Like copywriting, business writing is becoming more casual. Business writers no longer write, "The purpose of this memo is to ...," or "In regards to our conversation of March 15th ...," and other expressions we would never say in everyday conversation. It's a refreshing trend.

It is important to turn on the acetylene before turning on the oxygen. If the oxygen valve is turned on first, an explosion may occur.

On the other hand, a copywriter might write the same thing this way:

"A" before "O" — or up you'll go!

By the way, copywriting does not always involve catchy phrases and clever wordplays. In fact, the best copy I read gains attention simply, and then talks persuasively about the benefits of the product or service in a clear, interesting way.

Grammar

Copywriting can also differ from business writing in its use of grammar. It's been called the rebel son of business writing — and traditional English composition in general. Copywriters will unabashedly use colloquialisms, clichés, contractions, repetition, underlining, and italics to get their point across. Ads and brochures may be riddled with sentences starting with And, But, or Or. Sentence fragments are also common. Like this one.

Copywriters have always strived to make their writing conversational. Why? Because one-to-one conversations are the most persuasive form of communication. It's no accident that sales letters are so popular in direct mail and other marketing communications. They are direct and personal (even if they are mailed to thousands of people from the same list of names).

Visuals

Copywriting can also be a bit like screenwriting. A screenwriter will often "see" the movie playing in his or her head while writing the scenes. A copywriter does something similar. He or she will often "see" the ad or brochure while writing — visualizing how the artwork, headlines, and body copy work together to tell a persuasive story.

Ideas for artwork, visuals, and other graphical elements often pop into my head as I write. When this happens, I sketch out the idea and send it to my client or the designer (I can't draw, but I'm famous for my stickpeople). I may create a mocked-up version of the collateral I'm writing — folding and cutting paper, roughing in the headlines and images with a pencil — to help me better visualize what I'm writing.

The Demand for Good Copywriters

What does the future hold for copywriters? A lot of work! Most established, self-employed copywriters regularly turn down work. In fact, on the day I'm writing this, I had to turn down an assignment from a potential client because I was just too busy. I hate doing this because every business thrives on new clients (and turning them down makes me feel pretentious). But my current clients always come first.

Of course, I'm not immune to slow times and dips in business activity. No self-employed copywriter is. But you can rest assured there is a high demand for writers who can craft persuasive words, sentences, and paragraphs for effective advertising and marketing materials. If you're dedicated to learning the required skills and you can actively identify and attract clients, there is little reason why you won't be a busy professional for years to come.

There are a number of reasons why the demand for good copywriters is so high:

- *Continuous need for copy.* Businesses have an ongoing need to develop ads, brochures, websites, sales letters, press releases, articles, newsletters, and other collateral to promote their products and services. Business people often don't have the time, inclination, or skills to write the copy themselves, so they "outsource" to self-employed copywriters.

- *The growth of the Internet.* The growth of the Internet has created a new market for copywriters. When the medium first emerged, many people thought the days of printed brochures and direct-mail promotions were over. But did television replace radio, or even motion pictures? Hardly. These days, when I get an assignment to write a brochure, I get a *second* assignment to write copy for the website. In fact, developing content and writing copy for websites is now an important part of my business.

- *Shorter life cycles for materials.* The lifespan of sales and marketing materials has shrunk. This means more work, more often, from the same client. A few years ago, a brochure for

In her book *Freelance Copywriting*, British copywriter Diana Wimbs points out, "There's a huge market for copywriters and surprisingly few people to fill it. Why? Because many writers and would-be writers simply don't know such a market exists." Well, now you know.

an industrial gizmo would have had a useful life of five years. Now, it's trashed and redone within six months. (I wrote a series of brochures for a software company just seven months ago, and recently received an assignment to update every one.) Today's market moves fast, and customers want to see fresh, up-to-date material.

- *Downsizing of big business*. There was a time when many corporations and most ad agencies employed in-house writers. Those days are gone. After years of downsizing, businesses routinely farm out copy to freelance professionals (that's us) because they don't have the internal resources to handle the workload. Yes, downsizing has motivated many formerly employed copywriters to set up shop, which has increased competition. But the demand for copywriting services has outpaced available copywriters by a wide margin.

- *Writers don't know about the market*. There just aren't enough copywriters on the market to handle the demand. The reason? I suspect many prospective writers don't appreciate the potential of this business, or have little knowledge of copywriting in general.

The Road to Success

Copywriting is a surprisingly easy field to break into. Unlike writing a screenplay or a novel, you don't need to get that one-in-a-thousand lucky break. Copywriting is a business, and if you apply yourself, learn a few strategies, and stick with it, there is no reason why you cannot generate a solid income with your own copywriting business.

Everyone can come up with reasons why they won't be successful. For me it was age. I thought I was too old to switch from being a sales rep to becoming a self-employed copywriter. That was until I found out about David Ogilvy, perhaps the most famous copywriter of the 20th century. In advertising circles, he's a legend — but he didn't write a word of copy until he was 38 years old. Before that, he worked off and on as a salesperson, a diplomat, and even a farmer.

My road to becoming a self-employed copywriter was also not traditional. In university, I knew I loved to write. I also knew I enjoyed business. I just didn't put the two together. So, when I graduated with a degree in business, I drifted, eventually finding my way to sales.

I liked selling. As a technical sales representative, I often toured manufacturing plants in a variety of industries and found it fascinating to learn about new products and how they were made.

I also enjoyed the independence of a sales career. Although I was employed, I often worked solo and unsupervised. Because my income was a mix of salary and commission, I had more control over how much I earned. It was a little like being self-employed.

Yet, despite these advantages, I began to feel increasingly unsatisfied. Even though I was a top performer for a number of years — in fact, for three years in a row I held the record for signing new accounts — I developed a nagging feeling that a sales career was not for me. Confused, I began to flounder.

Then it happened. One day, the company I was working for decided to redesign its sales brochures. I was pleased. Most of the brochures were poorly written, some even painful to read. I gave them out to customers only reluctantly. My fellow reps often said they used the brochures only to show pictures of the products. I thought, "Shouldn't a sales brochure do more?"

Taking a breath, I marched into my sales manager's office and offered to write the new brochures. I gave him a song and dance on the few writing credentials I had, and assured him the task would not interfere with my selling duties. Much to my surprise, he said, "Yes." (In retrospect, he was probably not looking forward to writing the copy himself, and jumped at the chance of having the job lifted off his shoulders. Besides, my services were free.)

I don't remember a time when I approached a task more enthusiastically. I worked late into every evening on the brochures; weekends too. I coordinated my work with our graphic design firm, even hanging around the studio during the photo shoot. I admit I loved it. Although I knew little about copywriting (I didn't even know it was called copywriting) the brochures were received with unanimous applause around the company.

Then my carriage turned into a pumpkin, and I was back to life as a sales rep. But things had changed. Word of my writing skills spread through the company. First, the equipment division asked me to rewrite a proposal. Then the service manager enlisted my help

Freelance copywriter Bob Bly says in his book *Write More, Sell More*, "Freelance copywriting does not require a degree, certification, specific educational background, or work experience. The main qualification is the ability to write good copy."

on a particularly difficult customer letter. It didn't happen as often as I would have liked, but whenever people in the company had something challenging to write, they turned to me.

It wasn't long before I began learning everything I could about copywriting. I read every book I could find on the subject. Soon, I began to wonder if I could become a self-employed copywriter and work from a home office writing copy for clients.

Eventually, I began to build my copywriting business on a part-time basis — working many evenings and weekends to promote my services and complete copywriting assignments. The extra money I made went into a savings account to fund my eventual foray into full-time self-employment. This happy event occurred about three years later.

Over the years, I've built my reputation with a growing list of ad agency, design firm, and Fortune 500 corporate clients. I'm surprised at, and admittedly proud of, how fast I've managed to build my business to become among the top freelance copywriters in my market. If I can do it — starting with very little money, knowledge, or experience — with diligence and persistence, you can too.

You As a Self-Employed Copywriter

The road to success as a self-employed copywriter is not the same for everyone, but I am confident that success lies in wait for you if you try. I've seen too many people from so-called nontraditional backgrounds succeed in this business (myself included) to not believe that success is possible if you work hard.

Don't discount your life, education, and career experience — whatever it is. Some people mistakenly assume that all copywriters graduated with marketing degrees and plied their trade in advertising agencies before setting up shop as copywriters. This is true for some copywriters, but not for most. Many self-employed copywriters, in fact, have an astonishing variety of backgrounds. Some copywriters I know were once high-ranking marketing managers. Others drove trucks. Copywriter Alan Sharpe was a former British soldier and saw action in the Falklands war. Direct-mail specialist Ron Marshak taught economics.

Brenda Kruse comes from a more traditional background. A university graduate with a degree in advertising, she worked with several ad agencies before deciding to freelance. "I was approaching burnout at the agency," Brenda remembers, "and needed to make a change." She admits that venturing out on her own was scary, but today she is well niched as the "Farm Girl Copywriter" and works with major agri-marketing clients throughout the United States.

Copywriting may be a specialized field, but this book, as well as other books and resources I list on the CD-ROM, can help you learn what you need to succeed. So, if you love to write and enjoy business in general, you too can start and run a profitable copywriting business.

2
Is Having a Copywriting Business Right for Me?

Before getting your business cards printed, take a few moments to consider if being a self-employed copywriter is right for you. Of course, one of the advantages of the copywriting business is that you can easily start part time, thereby testing the water before you quit your day job and jump in. But before starting even part time, you may want to take a closer look at what it is like to be a copywriter and determine if the copywriting business is a good fit for you.

Like any self-employment opportunity, working as a freelance copywriter has unique advantages and disadvantages. Take a look at the pros and cons I've listed below. On the one hand, if the cons seem too hard to live with and the pros less tantalizing than expected, you might want to reconsider joining the ranks of self-employed copywriters. On the other hand, if you can live with the cons and the pros make you salivate for more, then the world of copywriting might be right up your ally.

Pros

The following are some of the advantages of being a self-employed copywriter.

Working from home

For most home-based business operators, working in the comfort of their home is a real advantage. Trust me, I don't miss rush hour or the endless interruptions and meetings inherent in most office environments. I have breakfast with my wife and daughter and then saunter up to my second-floor office in my slippers. I work productively, unfettered by roaming supervisors and office chatter. When a snowstorm hits, I watch it from my window and smile.

Self-employed copywriter Brenda Kruse says, "I enjoy the lower dry cleaning bills because I can dress casually ... I can run errands during the day when I need to ... even throw in a load of laundry during breaks in the day." Toronto copywriter Alan Sharpe says he sometimes takes walks through nearby woods for inspiration. Try doing that on Madison Avenue!

High income potential

It's unfortunate but, in survey after survey, freelance writers rank among the lowest paid professionals in North America. Freelance copywriters, on the other hand, are able to charge professional fees for professional work.

According to Adpeople Inc., an agency that represents creative professionals, copywriters can charge between $60 and $150 per hour, and sometimes more. Full-time, self-employed copywriters have little difficulty earning $50,000 annually, with many earning well into the six-figure range.

Of course, there is no guarantee as to how much *you* will earn as a self-employed copywriter. But there's no reason why you can't set your sights on achieving a good, professional income within the first year or two.

Low start-up costs

Initially, you can start your copywriting business with very little money. I did. I began with business cards, letterhead, and the best sales letter I could write. I sent those sales letters to 250 prospects gleaned from various business directories. Three weeks later, I got my first order from my first new client. And I'm proud of the fact that that client is still one of my clients today.

You will, of course, need some basic equipment, such as a desk, a computer, Internet access and an e-mail account, a telephone, and some basic office supplies. See Chapter 3 for more details on the start-up equipment needed.

Greater control over your work schedule

Notice I didn't say "Be your own boss." You'll have bosses, all right — plenty of them, if you're lucky. They're called clients. But as a freelancer, you will have greater control over your business life and working hours than if you were employed. For example, I'm more productive in the morning, so I start early — usually no later than 7:00 a.m. But by mid-afternoon my energy level fades. I use that time for scheduling client meetings, making phone calls, editing, and other activities that require less focused concentration.

You will, however, find that your schedule is rocked now and then by increased work flow, client demands, and deadlines. You may find yourself working evenings and weekends to complete a rush job for an important client. But this will ultimately be *your* decision.

Plenty of work to go around

In his book *Make It Your Business,* Stephan Schiffman says that having a market for your services is a crucial ingredient for success. "If customers are there, just about any other hurdle can be overcome. But if you're trying to sell something for which there's no market," Schiffman points out, "your business is doomed."

Thankfully, the market for copywriting services is huge. Consider the hundreds of thousands of advertising agencies, design firms, marketing companies, corporations, associations, government departments, and businesses — large and small — throughout North America: all potential clients. You only need a few to keep you busy and prosperous full time.

By using the Internet and online portfolios, many copywriters are doing a thriving business with clients throughout North America and around the world.

Working on creative, stimulating projects

One of the things I enjoy most about copywriting is the fascinating array of projects I get to work on. I'm naturally curious and easily bored, so I get a kick out of working on a website one day and creating an effective print ad the next. It's fun learning about new product and service innovations, often before the public gets wind of them. If you love to write and create, the copywriting business may be exactly what you're looking for.

Cons

Still interested in your own copywriting business? Great. But bear in mind the following down sides to the business before you make your decision.

Working from home

This isn't a mistake. I intentionally put "working from home" on both lists. Yes, working from home has its advantages — and for me the pros far outweigh the cons — but there are some drawbacks.

Most commonly considered a con is the solitude. If you like working with people — perhaps in a busy office environment filled with meetings, power lunches, and water-cooler chats with colleagues — then you'll find working from home to be quiet. Very quiet. You might meet with clients once or twice a month, but most of the time you'll be working alone. I like it, but it's not for everyone.

Lack of professional recognition

Successful self-employed copywriters are respected among their clients, colleagues, and the advertising and direct marketing industry. But attend a house party and tell someone what you do, and you might be greeted with, "What's that?" I've given up trying to describe my work to my parents. And when I told my sister how much I charge for a one-page sales letter, she almost fell to the floor.

Writing of any type is considered by many people to be a soft skill. You'll encounter professionals in other disciplines who do not understand the strategy and insights of copywriting. You might earn the same income as them (maybe more), but being a self-employed copywriter does not have the same status in mainstream society as an architect, lawyer, accountant, consultant, or plumber.

Uneven work flow

I know several professional speakers and admire their ability to book their seminars and speaking engagements months in advance. And when their schedule is full, it's full. The same cannot be said for copywriters. I have yet to receive an order in May that is due in September. Usually an order received in May is due in May (or sooner, if some clients could have their way).

Orders from clients tend to come in waves. Sometimes big waves. One week you're overloaded with all the business you can handle. The next, you're begging for the phone to ring.

The feast and famine roller coaster, especially during the first few years, can be stressful. To stay sane, you have to remember that clients do need your ongoing services — it may just be infrequent.

Deadline stress

Remember that English essay you had to write in the tenth grade? Remember how you felt as the due date approached? If you normally take a disciplined approach to completing tasks, then you'll handle deadline stress better than most. But if you're like the rest of us, tight deadlines can seem daunting.

Of course, you can always turn work down when you're busy, but that may be dangerous. What are you going to say when your best client calls and begs you to take on an extra project? If you say no, another copywriter is sure to get his or her foot in the door. And, when another project comes up, your "best client" may call that copywriter instead of you.

Most copywriters rank deadlines near the top of their list of stressors. I fight it in a number of ways: I plan my work the best I can, take a disciplined approach to completing tasks, and turn down work from potential new clients when I'm busy. (I *rarely* turn down work from a current client, and strongly suggest you don't.) I also reward myself after a particularly busy period with a few days off.

No published writing credit

This may affect your ego more if you're used to seeing your byline in articles and other pieces you have previously written for publication. As a copywriter, only you and your client will know who wrote the materials you worked so hard to scribe. Your name will not be anywhere on it.

"[Copywriting] is an ebb and flow business. I've gotten comfortable with the fact I may not have any work for a while, then a $5,000 order will fall on my lap."

— Copywriter Heather Lloyd-Martin

Once you commit to a deadline, never miss it. There are a lot of rules you can break in this business, but you can't break that one.

Copywriters work long hours at a computer. Good sitting posture, a comfortable work area, and regular exercise can help avoid wrist, back, and eye strain.

Copywriting is writing-for-hire in the strictest sense. Once your fee is paid, you have no further rights to the work. Your clients are free to rewrite, edit, republish, or reuse your words any way they wish. There are many websites that contain copy I had originally written for a brochure. The text was simply lifted from the brochure and pasted on the website. Do I mind? Not at all. But *you* might.

Your wrists, butt, waistline, and back

Copywriting exercises your mind, but not your body. By its nature, writing involves sitting and typing. Sure, you'll develop dextrous fingers, but your behind may spread in unwanted directions. And the fridge is temptingly close when you're working from home.

If you are going to be spending hours each day in front of a computer, you need to develop an exercise program. I like to take a short break every hour or so to get up, stretch, and walk around. I also exercise at a local gym (although less frequently than I care to admit). See Chapter 3 for suggestions on avoiding eye, back, and wrist strain.

No regular paycheck

It's obvious, but worth remembering. Once you become self-employed, your days of receiving a regular paycheck are over. No more Christmas bonuses. No more paid vacations. You may very well go weeks without any money coming in, and then open your mail and find three client checks worth thousands of dollars.

Your paychecks may not be regular, but as a self-employed professional, you'll have more control over how much — and how little — you earn than you ever had while employed. I can tell you from experience that earning a self-employed income is very empowering. I once rewarded myself with a new Nikon camera system after a particularly exhausting few weeks of working on client projects. I knew the effort that went into every cent I paid for that camera system. That was *my* Christmas bonus.

Financial stress in the first few years

When I asked copywriter Alan Sharpe what he liked *least* about the copywriting business he replied, "Number one, not being paid on time." In my experience, clients will usually pay your invoice 45 to 90 days after you send it. That's two to four months after you begin a project. So if you have a slow month in June, you're going to feel a cash flow crunch in September.

Before I started in this business, I was able to squirrel away an amount equal to six months of personal and business expenses as a cash reserve. But you may not be able to do the same thing. While you begin to establish yourself, your marketing expenses will be high, and client orders will tend to come in fits and starts. You may experience long lulls between projects. This is normal, but can be frightening and stressful.

A Day in the Life

You've probably heard of the Shadow Dad for a Day or Visit Mom at Work programs at school. Well, here's your chance to spend a day with me. Be my shadow, and see for yourself what a typical day may hold for *you* in the future.

Don't underestimate the difficulty of securing loans and insurance during your first few years as a self-employed professional. Lenders and insurers tend to be suspicious of self-employed income (perhaps for good reason). Before going solo as a copywriter, speak with a financial advisor.

7:00 a.m.

My usual starting time. After having breakfast with my family, I walk upstairs to my home office. As I turn on my computer I can still hear the sometimes distracting sounds of my wife and daughter getting ready for work and daycare. A friend of mine, also self-employed, has actually soundproofed his home office. I'm not willing to go that far. Personally, I enjoy working with the audible nuances of family life playing in the background. Much better, in fact, than the chatter of a busy office.

I check my e-mail and voice mail and review my schedule. I like to plan my work hour by hour as soon as I receive a client project. But a copywriter's schedule changes constantly. Today, my plans include working on a new brochure for an insurance company for most of the morning. In the afternoon, I will read background materials and make notes on a new website I'm writing for a software firm.

As I look out my home office window, I can see my wife and daughter pulling out of the driveway. I wave.

Now, the house is quieter, and I begin to write. I write about half a page as quickly as I can. Then I go over it, fix it up, polish it here and there, and move on. I use this simple but effective writing system as I make my way through the brochure.

I prefer that clients send me background materials that I can mark up with a pen or highlighter. If they send me something they want returned, I make a photocopy.

9:00 a.m.

After two hours, I have completed a clean rough draft. It's far from finished. There is still a lot of improving, editing, and massaging to do. I may completely rewrite entire passages, but the essence of the brochure is there in words — and this is a lot less stressful to work with than a blank screen.

I take a break, stretch, and get a coffee. Jill, the manager of client services for an advertising agency in the city, calls. She's one of my better clients. "Steve, I'm sorry I didn't call you earlier," Jill begins, "but we landed a new client last Friday. And they want us to put together a series of brochures. The time frame is tight. Can you possibly make a brainstorm session tomorrow afternoon?"

Off-site meetings with clients are not an everyday occurrence for self-employed copywriters. I attend such meetings no more than three or four times a month. Most project information, in fact, can be exchanged by e-mail, fax, couriers, phone calls, and conference calls. But when I do get a request from a good client to meet, I usually agree.

We set our meeting for 2:30 p.m. tomorrow. I always try to schedule meetings for mid-afternoon, because this maximizes my writing time for the rest of the day. I've found that when I attend a meeting any earlier in the day, I have trouble getting back into the writing groove when I return to my office.

9:15 a.m.

I take a few minutes to readjust my plans for the day. Because I feel comfortable with my progress on the brochure, I decide to dedicate the remainder of the morning to reviewing the background materials for a website I'm writing.

As I go through the mountain of documents my client sent me — old brochures, press releases, ads, memos, proposals — I freely highlight, circle, and make side notes while culling the key benefits, unique advantages, and other important information needed to make the website effective.

12:00 noon

I take a break at lunch, go downstairs, and fix myself a sandwich. One of the things I love about being self-employed is working in the comfort of home. I don't have to line up at a busy restaurant or eat a meal at my desk. I can relax at the kitchen table, read the paper, or watch the news.

12:30 p.m.

A half hour later I return to my office and continue on the website.

1:30 p.m.

The phone rings. The caller is the marketing manager of a mid-sized technology firm. He explains he was given my name by one of my current clients and says, "We have a direct-mail package we need put together to generate leads for our sales staff. But, before we go any further, could you send us some information on your services, and perhaps some samples of your work?"

I thank him for his call and tell him I would be delighted to have an opportunity to quote on his project. I make it a point to put together the information he needs, so it can be mailed today. I also make a note to thank my current client for the referral.

2:00 p.m.

I make some follow-up calls on leads and inquiries I've received over the past couple of weeks. I also take some time to review a postcard mailing I'm planning to send to marketing managers of key software firms. Although my workload is generally full, I schedule time each day for marketing and other business activities. I'm busy. And I want to stay busy.

2:30 p.m.

I've been working on the website for a while today and my energy level is starting to ebb. I decide to switch gears and begin work on an Internet direct-mail piece I'm writing for a major client. Internet direct mail — which is not to be confused with spam e-mail — is very similar to a sales letter. I love writing these, and enjoy the challenge.

4:00 p.m.

My day is almost over. I clear my desk, sketch out my work plan for tomorrow, and notice that an e-mail has come in. It reads:

"Hi Steve. We all liked the work you did on the sales letter and brochure package. We made some comments on a couple of sections, however. Could you take a look at these and get back to us in the morning? Thanks, Bill."

There is a file attached. I open it and review the comments Bill and his team have made. Pretty minor, mainly concerning content. I e-mail him back saying I'll schedule time tomorrow to call them and that I can have a revised version to them within two business days.

On another project — a small sales brochure nearing completion — I make a call to the designer and ask if she can send me a PDF of the layout by e-mail. Portable document format (PDF) files, used with Adobe Acrobat and Adobe Acrobat Reader, are a common way to view graphic files across different computer platforms. I work on a PC, but most designers use Macs. The designer agrees to send me the file and says, "It's a work in progress. Please give me your opinion of the layout." In my experience, the more closely I can work with the designer, the better the results for my client.

4:15 p.m.

Time to pick up my daughter. It's been a great day.

Typical day? I admit, this one does sound a bit idyllic. Some days are much more hectic, especially if the day includes travel to a client meeting. But it's not too far off the mark — and similar, I suspect, to the workdays of many busy copywriters.

Can you see yourself spending your day this way? Or do the writing tasks, solitude, and client demands I describe seem overwhelming? Only you can decide.

Use Checklist 1 to help you determine if running your own copywriting business is for you. The checklist is based on the characteristics I've found to be common among most self-employed copywriters I have interviewed. It's far from scientific, but it will give you an idea of the skills and attributes necessary to succeed in this business.

Checklist 1
IS A FREELANCE COPYWRITING BUSINESS RIGHT FOR ME?

Check AGREE or DISAGREE to the following statements:	AGREE	DISAGREE
1. I enjoy working independently, rather than on a team.	❏	❏
2. I enjoy working in solitude, rather than in a busy office.	❏	❏
3. I love to write and actually enjoy working on even the toughest writing tasks. I take pride in writing well.	❏	❏
4. I think visually and often see pictures and images as I write.	❏	❏
5. I am somewhat motivated by money. I get great satisfaction from being paid well for what I do.	❏	❏
6. I have a burning desire to be self-employed. Despite the risks, I prefer it to having a "real job."	❏	❏
7. I have some advertising, sales, and/or marketing experience OR I am interested in learning more about these topics.	❏	❏
8. I have some writing samples (sales letters, articles, web pages, blog entries) that I can show to prospective clients.	❏	❏
9. I have experience as a staff writer for a business, a nonprofit, a PR firm, or an agency.	❏	❏
10. I can handle some financial pressure. An unpredictable cash flow is a concern, but doesn't alarm me.	❏	❏
11. I am reasonably self-motivated and disciplined. I get things done without supervision.	❏	❏
12. I enjoy working with business clients.	❏	❏

Checklist 1 — Continued

	AGREE	DISAGREE
13. I don't consider myself an artist who is "selling out" by doing copywriting on a for-profit basis.	☐	☐
14. I can communicate effectively by phone, e-mail, and in meetings.	☐	☐
15. I have a quiet, comfortable, and functional place to work (with computer, phone, and Internet access).	☐	☐
16. I have little desire to manage or supervise other people.	☐	☐
17. I have little desire to be managed or supervised.	☐	☐
18. I have been exploring the field of copywriting and find the subject fascinating.	☐	☐
19. I am reasonably confident that I can meet deadlines and other commitments I make with clients.	☐	☐
20. I can write on a schedule. I don't need to wait for "inspiration."	☐	☐

So, how did you do? If you checked AGREE with 9 or more of the above, I would guess you have a fairly good shot at making it in the copywriting business. If you checked AGREE to 12 or more, your chances of success as a freelance copywriter are excellent! If, however, you agreed with fewer than 5 of the above points, you may need to take a close look at whether life as a self-employed copywriter is really for you.

By the way, don't worry if you checked DISAGREE to a few of these points. I did. The fact is, if you love to write and have a desire to be self-employed, most of the other traits can be learned or overcome. It's up to you.

3
Getting Started

Ready to get started? Great! Let's take a look at some of the things you will need to launch your new copywriting business (or kick-start your current freelance copywriting efforts).

The great thing about this business is that you can start reasonably small and accumulate your office supplies, sales materials, resources, and other necessities as you go. What I recommend in this chapter are minimums, but I also suggest items you will likely want to invest in as your business grows and matures.

A note about costs: I have done my best to give you the most educated estimates I can based on my experience as a freelance copywriter in the greater Toronto area. Costs in your area, however, are bound to differ. Use my numbers as a rough guide to help you budget.

Your personal needs, preferences, and ambitions will greatly affect your start-up costs. I suggest you start modestly, but if you

Start your business small and accumulate your office supplies, sales materials, and resources as you go along.

have the money and inclination to set up a fancy office, design an elaborate website, and have reams of expensive letterhead printed, go for it. Just remember, this isn't a necessity.

When I started my copywriting business, my wife and I were waiting for our home to be built (which, because of labor strikes, took more than a year). In the interim, we lived in a small condominium apartment where I worked out of a little office not much bigger than a closet. There was barely enough room to fit a desk, let alone a copywriter. Yet I managed to complete some of my first paid copywriting assignments in that little room and built the beginnings of my client base. So, yes, you certainly can start small.

Focus on a Goal

This isn't a motivational book on goal setting. However, I strongly suggest you set clear short-term and long-term goals for your copywriting business. In his popular book *Seven Habits of Highly Effective People*, Stephen Covey says, "Begin with the end in mind." Good advice. In my experience, without a clear picture of where you want to go, it's all too easy to waste time spinning your wheels.

I'm hardly an expert on goal setting. In fact, I admit my history of setting and achieving goals is shaky. Sometimes I feel I got where I am more by accident than by design. But the times I felt most energized and motivated were when I set out to achieve a clearly defined goal.

Author and sales coach Tom Stoyan suggests writing your goals down and reviewing them at least once a month. Because I spend so much time at my computer, I keep my goals in a computer folder named Goals and review them frequently. Inside my Goals folder are four separate files: 90-day goals, one-year goals, three-year goals, and overall goals.

My 90-day goals tend to be very specific. Among my 90-day goals for this quarter, for example, are to attract another Fortune 500 corporate account, get another major mail-order copywriting assignment, and ride my bike around Lake Simcoe (a goal I set before I realized how big Lake Simcoe was).

My three-year goals and overall goals tend to be less specific and more lofty. One of my overall goals, for example, is to be an outstanding father. One of my three-year goals is to be among the top

2 percent of successful freelance copywriters in my two target markets: marketing managers of business-to-business Fortune 500 corporations and direct-mail marketers. Because I market my services to these specific groups, it's easier for me to gauge how I stack up against other freelance copywriters in the same markets.

When I began my copywriting business, I didn't define many goals and tended to drift. Don't make the same mistake I did. Set some milestones you want to hit within the first few months and years of your copywriting business. Write them down and review them often. Remember: goals evolve. You can, and I'm sure you will, change them as you go along.

Ask yourself: "Where do I want my business to be in three months? A year? Three years?" Your three-month goal might be to get your business up and running and secure your first copywriting client. Your one-year goal might be an income objective — to consistently invoice $3,000 per month, for example.

I like to think of goals as a road map. There's always a way to get from where you are to where you want to go. You merely have to find the best route. Just remember, as with any journey, you are bound to encounter bumps in the road, hitchhikers, bad weather, and unexpected obstacles, and at times you're going to run out of gas. But I firmly believe that if you keep your destination in sight, you'll eventually get there.

One last note about goal setting: Don't forget to celebrate when you reach a milestone. When I was starting out, I worked hard to win that first major corporate-writing assignment. When I did, I got my wife to take a photo of me proudly holding the purchase order. That picture is still pinned to my bulletin board where I can see it each day. It's quite motivating. (And the company that gave me that order is still one of my clients.)

Are You Going to Start Part Time or Full Time?

Part time is a great way to launch your copywriting business, and I do recommend it. However, it can create conflicts with other priorities. For example, if you have another job during the day, how are you going to contact clients and complete assignments? If you are a busy parent with small children at home, how are you going to handle

Your goals will be unique to you, based on your priorities and ambitions. I know a copywriter who set this one-year goal for herself: "Consistently earn $2,500 per month while maintaining a flexible schedule and free time for my son." She achieved that goal.

a crying child while you're struggling to meet a deadline or you're on the phone with an important client? Careful planning is crucial.

The key advantage of working part time is financial. If you have another source of income, then you avoid many of the financial pressures associated with starting a business. You can start small, make some mistakes, grow your client base at your own pace, and not get too stressed by cash-flow headaches.

Setting up a full-time copywriting business is a much different experience. Financial demands increase dramatically but, in many ways, it's easier than working part time. You have fewer conflicts because your business is a priority, not just a sideline.

You'll also be taken more seriously by clients when you're working full time. You can attend client meetings at any time of the day, and can freely schedule the time you need to complete client work. When I quit my job and went out on my own as a self-employed copywriter, my business tripled in the first month. The reason? I was putting all my energy, full time, toward making the business work.

However, you'll likely experience some financial worries from time to time, especially if you are relying on your copywriting business to generate some or all of your personal income needs. Financial stress is part of any new business venture, and there's not much you can do about it. Just plan well, carefully monitor your cash flow, and try not to get too many gray hairs.

Playing the Name Game

The Write Touch … Write for Business … The Write Words … The Right Writer … Writing that's Right … No doubt you've seen names like these before, especially among freelance writers, copywriters, and business writers. There is nothing wrong with creating a business name that plays on the curious fact that "right" is pronounced the same as "write." It has just been overdone.

Coming up with a creative, unique business name is difficult. In fact, some corporations and start-ups pay consultants tens of thousands of dollars to do just that. I recently read an article about a firm that charges $100,000 to find a name for a corporation. One name!

I've had a long adventure with business names over the years. One of my earlier creations was word/vision. The perfect name; I'm a genius, I thought. Until one day I was networking at a trade show and everyone thought I worked for WorldVision Canada, a well-known charity.

Then I got it into my head that calling myself a "copywriter" was too uninspired. So I adopted the title of "Promotional Writer" and included it on all my letterhead and business cards. Brilliant, I thought. I'll stand out from the crowd. And I certainly did. Within weeks I had received inquiries ranging from someone wanting me to run an employee incentive program, to an auto dealer asking if I could rent him a large floating gorilla for a weekend sales blitz he was planning. (I had no idea how he connected Promotional Writer to promotional balloons. And I didn't care. I dropped the name.)

Expect your business name to change as your business evolves.

For a couple of years, I was known by the business name, "The Writing Project." Not bad as names go, but I was never comfortable with it. It didn't sound like me and it created confusion. Some people thought I offered writing seminars. Others commented that the name sounded like academia, not business. So eventually, I began to market my services simply as "Steve Slaunwhite, Copywriting/Consulting."

The funny thing is, once I began to market my services under my own name, my business improved. I discovered that agency executives and corporate marketing professionals were far more interested in Steve Slaunwhite the copywriter than the business name I used. In fact, when I hid behind a business name, I would sometimes get confused for a mortar-and-brick type business, not the independent professional most clients were interested in hiring. So *Steve Slaunwhite, Copywriting/Consulting* it was and has remained.

If you do decide to use a business name — rather than your name — expect that name to change as your business evolves. I know very few self-employed professionals who have kept the same business name they started with. You may find within a few years that your business has gone down an unexpected road, and the business name you are using isn't appropriate anymore. You might want to think about this before you invest in your initial supply of business cards and letterhead. (I still have reams of The Writing Project stationery, and use it for scrap paper.)

Business Cards and Letterhead

Business cards and letterhead are a necessity for any business. You'll need business cards to trade with clients and prospects. Imagine how clients will react if they ask you for a business card, and you don't have one? You'll also need letterhead to write sales letters, invoices, and other client correspondence. Without professional-looking stationery, few people will take you seriously.

I have seen lots of effective business cards — some jazzy and daring, others plainer and more conservative. I suggest you go with a business card design that is simple and effective. You can always invest in more complex designs, or even a logo, as your business matures.

Copywriter Alan Sharpe, in his article "How to Find and Work with a Professional Copywriter," actually warns clients of inkjet business cards that rub off on your fingers. Potential clients, especially ad agencies, are wary of the fly-by-night crowd. If your business card looks cheap, they won't give you a second look. Worse, you may be forever labeled in their minds as an amateur. Believe me, minds can be difficult to change.

A simply designed business card and letterhead doesn't mean cheap. Be sure to use a professional designer (unless you happen to be a very good designer yourself) and get your stationery printed on high-quality stock. Never yield to the temptation of buying those business card templates available in most office supply stores, and printing cards with your inkjet printer. This is *not* suitable for the professional image you need to convey. And no "bubblegum machine" business cards, please. In my local shopping mall there is a kiosk in the main hallway. For $10 you can punch in your name and other information, pick a template, and print out 100 business cards. No, no, no.

Michael Huggins, a graphic design professional and president of MindWalk Design Group of Toronto, says, "Expect to pay at least $1,000 to $1,500 for a good business card and stationery design. Of course, less experienced designers will charge you less, but will have less expertise and require more direction." And be sure to show your designer samples of business cards and stationery you like. That way, he or she will be able to create a design that best appeals to you and fits your business needs. Design, by the way, does not include printing costs. That is extra.

Planning Your Work Space

I once received a sales letter from a freelance copywriter offering a cassette program on — what else? — becoming a successful free-lance copywriter. He described in blissful terms the wonderful life he leads sitting by his swimming pool each day, getting a tan, and writing copy for his blue-chip slate of clients.

Sounds idyllic, but I suspect very few successful self-employed professionals work this way. (I once tried working on my patio and I got too distracted.) Most copywriters I know work standard business hours in well-equipped, comfortable home offices.

As a copywriter, you're going to be spending a lot of time in front of a computer, so I can't emphasize enough how important it is to create a pleasant, productive work environment for yourself. If that happens to be by the pool, great. Just make sure it's quiet, efficient, and comfortable.

When setting up a home office or any work area in your home, make sure it is dedicated to your business. This is especially true if you intend to use your home office as a tax deduction. Most tax jurisdictions will not allow you to write off a home office that doubles for another purpose. Canadian Income Tax Interpretation Bulletins, for example, specifically state that a home office is not deductible if it has a bed in it (so there's no tax advantage to the popular guest bedroom/den combination).

There are other reasons why you should strive to make your home office as dedicated and private as possible. For example, if your office doubles as the rec room, what if you're working late and your kids have scheduled a ping-pong game? Or a pajama party? If your desk is in your bedroom, what if your spouse is taking a nap just when you want to get some work done?

Of course, if you already have a room in your home designated as the home office, you have an advantage. If you don't, and no room in your home is available to be used exclusively as an office, then you'll have to get a little creative. I know someone who converted an oversized closet into a very comfortable (but admittedly small) office. You might have a similar nook in your home that you can adapt.

Shop around for specialty desks that cater to home office workers with space challenges. I've seen several that look like decorative wall units or corner hutches. With a few pulls and tugs these units morph into highly efficient office centers with plenty of desk space and space for a computer and phone. When your work is finished, you simply close them up again. Because of their design and complexity, however, the prices for these units tend to be high.

Of course, you might consider renting office space outside your home. This can be very costly, and I wouldn't recommend it — at

Buy all the computer you can afford. Get the highest speed, most robust features, lots of memory, and the latest software. Many clients you'll be dealing with will have the latest technology. They expect you to be just as up-to-date.

least not until your copywriting business is firmly established and generating a consistent monthly income.

If you decide to rent office space, monitor the classified section of your newspaper. Sometimes leasors of large office suites will sublet one of their private offices to a self-employed professional — often to offset their own costs. In fact, you may know a business owner with a spare office who might be willing to do just that.

The small-business office co-op is another alternative. These are office suites that are home to several small businesses that share common expenses such as meeting rooms, phone lines, Internet servers, and sometimes even a receptionist. In tight markets, they often have waiting lists. Check out the classifieds under "Office/Commercial Space" for co-op office ads.

You Must Have a Computer

You won't get far as a freelance copywriter without a computer. In fact, you won't get anywhere. No client I know of accepts typewritten copy anymore.

If you don't currently own a computer, your first decision will be "laptop or desktop?" A laptop computer takes up less space than a desktop does and is, of course, portable. But a good desktop model is more comfortable to work on.

The good news about purchasing a computer is that the technology is maturing, and prices are constantly tumbling. In this morning's newspaper, I noticed a flyer from my computer manufacturer offering a model with virtually the same features I have now — at half the lease price. And I leased my computer from this company just a year ago!

You'll find, when spending hours at a computer, that little enhancements make a big difference. When I leased my computer, I paid extra for an ergonomically shaped keyboard. It looks odd, but is tremendously more comfortable and a lot easier on my hands and wrists than a conventional keyboard. When my conventional mouse broke, I purchased a cordless mouse as a replacement. Now, instead of fighting with a cord, I easily and effortlessly move the cordless mouse and can place it anywhere on my desk. I also invested extra money in a 19-inch monitor that is great for clarity and easy on my eyes, and enables me to view two pages at once, which is handy.

Mac or PC? I choose a PC because that's what I started with. Virtually all advertising agencies use Macs, but can convert PC files with little problem. And most of my corporate clients use PCs. If you already own a Mac, stay with it. Your ad agency accounts will love you. And, with products like Adobe Acrobat and other software innovations, I find that the problems of sharing files across different platforms is becoming a thing of the past.

Sample 1 outlines some of the equipment you may consider buying to set up your home office for your copywriting business.

You Must Have Internet Access and an E-Mail Account

E-mail will be the most important communication tool you'll use in your copywriting business. It's as indispensable as the telephone. Virtually all the copy I write is submitted to my clients by e-mail. In fact, I don't remember the last time I mailed, couriered, or faxed a hard copy to a client. I believe those days are gone.

Fortunately, Internet access and e-mail are relatively inexpensive to set up. I've seen plans advertised for as little at $4.95 per month for dial-up access. And e-mail accounts are free at such online services as Yahoo! and Hotmail.

I strongly suggest that you get the highest speed Internet access you can. Preferably broadband or cable. Why? Clients are increasingly sending background materials to copywriters as e-mail file attachments ... and some of these files can be quite large. I once had a client send me a 3MB PowerPoint presentation by e-mail while I was on the phone! He expected me to receive it, open it, and discuss it with him *at that moment*. If I had slow dial-up access, the e-mail would have taken several minutes to receive. Fortunately, with my trusty high-speed connection, I had the presentation received, opened, and ready to discuss *in seconds.*

What Happens When the Phone Rings?

Many home-based professionals use their personal phone line for their business, but I don't recommend it. It creates too many problems, and there is always the risk of a potential client catching you in the act of being unprofessional. For example, what if your teenage daughter gets on the phone just when an important client

Make sure your Internet service provider has a reputation for reliable connections — especially during peak periods. There is nothing more frustrating than trying to send an e-mail to an important client and not being able to connect because of busy signals.

Sample 1
COPYWRITER'S OFFICE SETUP

Computer

This is a must. Make sure your computer has plenty of memory so you can store large graphics files and view electronically published materials sent to you by clients. My computer has 40 GBS of memory on the hard drive, plus 520MB of RAM (Random Access Memory). Don't let the technical terms intimidate you. Just make sure you ask your computer dealer for a machine that is capable of running a *professional* version of a major office suite application (such as *Microsoft Office*). Chances are, he'll show you the computer you need.

Get a big monitor. Trust me, you don't want to squint at a 14-inch screen for hours on end. This will only lead to fatigue and eye strain. I suggest investing in a 15-inch or even a 17-inch monitor with a flat screen. These have the highest resolution for crisp, clear text.

Estimated cost: $750 to $2,500

Printer

You'll mostly be e-mailing your copy to clients, rather than sending them a hard copy on paper, so your choice of printer is not that critical. Still, you'll want one that is fast and relatively quiet, and produces good quality print. After all, you may be running off sales letters, invoices, and other prospect/client communications on this machine. I suggest a laser printer if you want the best quality. Most are less than $1,000.

Estimated cost: $250 to $750

Scanner

A scanner creates a copy of whatever it scans and puts it on your computer screen. It's handy, but optional. I use it to scan the text of documents I receive from clients so I don't have to retype them into my computer. I have a special software that converts the text images into editable text files. It saves me time.

Estimated cost: $50 to $250

Sample 1 — Continued

Fax machine

Here's a technology that keeps hanging on. I still receive five to ten faxes a week and, despite having e-mail and most of my documents — invoices, samples, quotes — available in electronic formats, I still find I need to fax something at least once a week.

Fax machines are relatively inexpensive these days. You can also buy software so you can send and receive faxes on your computer.

Estimated cost: $100 to $250

Tip: If space is a problem, consider purchasing an all-in-one machine. You can fax, scan, print, and copy with just one machine!

Software

Office Suite. I suggest you invest in a professional version of a major office suite software package, such as *Microsoft Office* or *WordPerfect Office*. These will give you everything you need to write documents, view images, open presentations sent to you by clients, store contact information for mailing lists, and even build a website.

Estimated cost: $500 to $950

Adobe Acrobat. This software allows you to view files saved in portable document format (PDF) across different computer platforms. For example, if a designer uses a Mac computer and you use a PC, Adobe Acrobat lets you view graphic files from the designer that you would normally not be able to open on a PC. You can download a free version of Acrobat Reader from the Internet. This version lets you view PDF documents, but not edit them. I recommend buying the full version of Adobe Acrobat as you will then be able to edit the files and create your own PDF files. (Visit <www.Adobe.com> for more details.)

Estimated cost: $240 to $300

Contact management software. As your business grows, so will your contact base. Contact management software allows you to quickly and easily update contact information. I use my contact management software — *Act!* — to manage my client list and prospect list, remind me of people to call and things to do, and schedule my work. Another popular contact management brand is Maximizer.

Estimated cost: $250 to $750

Bookkeeping/accounting software. I cannot emphasize enough the importance of keeping an accurate, up-to-date set of financial books for your copywriting business. Fortunately, there are plenty of software products that make the task a lot easier — even if you have no previous bookkeeping or accounting experience. I use *QuickBooks* Pro, which allows me to enter my receipts and invoices while the software automatically updates all my accounts and creates income statements and balance sheets. Other popular accounting software include *Simply Accounting* and *MYOB Accounting*.

Estimated cost: $150 to $250

Desk

I have two desks: One is a traditional desk where I use the phone and do manual paperwork tasks; the other, my computer desk, is set up with my computer for optimal safety and comfort. You don't need two desks (the second is a luxury and convenience), but I do suggest you invest in a large, good-quality computer desk designed for comfort and efficiency while you ply your trade for long hours at the computer.

Estimated cost: $250 and up.

Chair

Copywriters spend a lot of time sitting, so it makes sense to have a comfortable chair. I suggest a pivoting, swiveling office chair with arms to rest your elbows as you type. Investigate ergonomically designed chairs that are specially made with spine and back health in mind. Spending a little extra here can go a long way to avoid potential back problems in the future.

Estimated cost: $250 and up.

Filing cabinet

Clients are going to send you a lot of paper: old brochures, creative briefs, memos, marked-up copy drafts, technical reports, transcriptions of customer interviews, market research reports — the works. I have seven file folders thick with inserts for just one of my clients. You will also need filing space for your own business records and other information. I suggest at least a four-drawer, legal-size filing cabinet. It's working well for me (although mine is getting full and I may have to purchase a second soon).

Estimated cost: $200 to $450

Tape recorder with telephone adapter

When writing case studies, annual reports, features, success stories, and other marketing documents, you may have to conduct in-depth interviews with your clients; your client's customers, stakeholders, and employees; and others involved in the project. I'm terrible at taking notes, so I use a tape recorder. Mine has an adapter so I can record phone interviews (and I always ask the other caller for permission before recording a phone conversation — this is the law in some jurisdictions). I suggest you buy a compact tape recorder that uses mini-cassettes, which is easier to carry, less cumbersome, and less obtrusive during face-to-face interviews. (**Tip**: Always have extra batteries and cassette tapes on hand. You don't want to face the embarrassment of running out during an interview.)

Estimated cost: $100 to $300

is trying to reach you? Worse, what if your three-year-old (like *my* three-year-old) is in the habit of answering the phone when it rings? Some of your clients might think it's cute. Others won't. Why take the risk?

I suggest you invest in a second phone line — for *business use only*. That way, when the phone rings, everyone in your household will know it's a business call, and will react accordingly.

A separate phone line for your business also allows you to record a more business-appropriate message for your voice mail or answering machine. Clients will have a tough time taking you seriously if your voice mail message is, "This is the Robertson family and Janice Robertson, copywriter. No one is home right now …"

I'm amazed that so many home-based professionals pay so little attention to their recorded voice mail message. For prospective clients, it could very well be the first time they hear your voice.

Here's the voice mail message I recorded today:

"Hi, you've reached the office of Steve Slaunwhite for Monday, May 30th. Sorry I missed your call. I'm in the office all day today so I'm likely on the phone or away from my desk at the moment. Please leave a message at the sound of the tone, and I promise I'll return your call at the first opportunity. And thanks for calling."

Start-Up Finances

How much money will you need to get started? Before I made the move to full-time self-employment, I read many books on the subject. The general consensus is that you should have the equivalent of six months' salary and three months' anticipated business expenses in the bank before you make the leap. I recommend you have 9 to 12 months' savings. The more cash you have in reserve, the less desperate you are going to feel.

Why do you need a healthy bank account before you start your business? Chances are, it's going to take some months before you realize a consistent personal income from your freelancing efforts. It takes time to find and establish clients, send invoices, and receive checks from clients. In the interim, you have rent or mortgage payments, bills, and business expenses.

Update your recorded message each day — clients seem to appreciate it. Try to sound cheerful and professional, and always include your schedule for the day so they know if you're away from the office, or just temporarily away from the phone.

When I was ready to quit my day job and run my copywriting business on a full-time basis, I was fortunate to have set aside six months in personal and business expenses. But, in addition to this, I also had the beginnings of a strong client base from my part-time efforts, a fully equipped office, marketing materials, and business cards. If I was starting from scratch, with no office or clients, it would have been a much tougher go.

"But I don't have six months' cash in the bank," you might say. "Can I still start my copywriting business?" Of course you can. I know many people who have started with nothing and built successful home-based businesses. But it's not easy, and it is financially stressful — especially if you have no other sources of income. It can be done, but if there is any way you can start part time while keeping your day job, or start full time with some money saved in a contingency fund, you will be much better off.

Even if you kick off your copywriting business with a couple of quick assignments, it takes time to get paid. You'll need to complete those assignments. That could take several days or even weeks. Then you have to invoice your client. Then you have to wait for the client to send you a check. How long do clients take to pay? Regardless of the terms of your invoice, in my experience it takes 45 to 90 days for a client to process your invoice and send payment, sometimes longer. Sixty days is average. So, by the time you receive any money from a particular copywriting job, three or four months can easily slip by.

Sample 2 shows a typical start-up budget for most copywriters starting a business from scratch. The costs are my best estimates; your actual costs will vary. Use this as a guide to plan your own budget.

Assuming you need to purchase everything in the sample budget, you will require $6,545 plus a six-month reserve for personal income needs to fund the start of your full-time copywriting business. This includes your start-up costs of $3,950 and three months' business expenses ($865 x 3). In my opinion, if you are starting with no clients, these amounts are a minimum.

Of course, if you're starting your business part time — and have other sources of income — you may not need as large of a cash reserve. But you will still have start-up costs and will need to fund business expenses until you achieve a consistent level of income.

Remember to plan for the start-up costs discussed in this chapter, as well as the plethora of "little" expenses you will incur that you can't begin to predict now. Those little expenses add up.

Sample 2
START-UP BUDGET

Here is a sample budget based on setting up a copywriter's office with just the basics. As your business grows, you can gradually add a filing cabinet, scanner, bookshelf, and other provisions.

Start-up costs

Business cards, letterhead, and other stationery (design and printing)	$ 1,000
Computer	$ 1,500
Printer	$ 500
Basic office supplies	$ 250
Office desk and chair	$ 750
Telephone and initial connection fee	$ 200
Total	**$ 4,200**

Anticipated monthly business expenses

Internet service and e-mail account (high-speed access)	$ 50
Telephone	$ 50
Car expense or public transit (visiting clients)	$ 150
Office supplies (monthly replenishment)	$ 100
Sales, marketing, self-promotion	$ 500
Miscellaneous	$ 150
Total	**$ 1,000**

The great thing about the copywriting business, like any writing pursuit, is that you can start very modestly. You don't need to have everything I list in this chapter in place before you begin your business. You can start with a phone, computer, and some stationery and build from there, accumulating other software, hardware, and office furnishings as you go along. After all, the most important thing you need to get started is a demonstrated ability to write copy.

4
Building Your Book

My first meeting with a prospective copywriting client was at a public relations agency that specialized in the automotive industry. Up to that point in my fledgling copywriting career, I had never had a paid copywriting assignment. In fact, I had not been inside a public relations agency.

I walked into the director of client services' office, sat across from him at his desk, and tried to look as enthusiastic as possible. He could see I was nervous. He leaned back in his chair, laced his fingers behind his neck, smiled, and said, "Okay, son. Let me see your book."

"Book?" I mumbled. "What book?"

What Is a Book?

Chances are, you're not as ignorant as I was when I started in this business, but if you don't know what a "book" is, you are forgiven.

In advertising circles, your portfolio of work samples is referred to as your "book."

In fact, "book" is a colloquialism that means different things in different industries. In musical theater, for example, the "book" is the story. In the training and development industry, "book" means schedule. So when corporate trainers talk about having a full book, they mean they have a full schedule.

In advertising and marketing, a "book" is a portfolio of samples. This is what you show prospective clients so they can learn more about the creative work you have done. Books are often filled with samples of advertisements, sales letters, direct-mail packages, brochures, and any other collateral a particular copywriter has had a hand in creating.

If you come from an ad agency background, you know all about books. You've likely seen dozens of them from colleagues, applicants for employment, and freelance creatives with whom the agency has worked. (A "creative" is a catch-all term used by the advertising industry to describe designers, illustrators, and copywriters.)

Typically, books are put together in large black portfolio cases that, when open, take up the better part of a conference table. They come with several large, clear plastic insert pages for holding and displaying samples.

In advertising circles, a strong book is considered a ticket to employment. In fact, many agency executives will hire a young creative based exclusively on his or her book and little else. It's seen as a clear demonstration of a copywriter's, designer's, or illustrator's ability to develop concepts and execute creative ideas through to production.

Curiously, having a strong book filled with great samples is not as important when seeking freelance copywriting work. As a self-employed professional offering copywriting services, ad agency executives or corporate marketing managers are interested in the services you can provide to their projects. They want to know what you can do, not what you have done. This doesn't mean you shouldn't have a solid book of samples to show. You definitely should — it's a great selling tool. But be prepared to also demonstrate your approach to solving marketing problems, your commitment and ability to follow through, how easy you are to work with, and the value you can add to a particular project. I have often received assignments from new clients based solely on the sales letter and information kit I sent them and by chatting with them about their requirements over the phone, without ever having shown my book.

As a self-employed copywriter, you are more likely to experience a thorough review of your book from an ad agency executive than from a direct client. And since many of your clients will probably be ad agencies, putting together the most impressive book you can will boost your marketing efforts.

I admit, I have mixed feelings about the book, especially about how many copywriters present their samples to potential clients. Some copywriters, in fact, expect their book to do all the work in a presentation to a prospective client. One copywriter I know insists her book does all the talking for her. "I don't have to say anything," she says, "my book says it all." But I suspect she would be much more successful if she did say something more about the services she offers.

Build the best book of samples you can, but never forget there are many other factors that contribute to a client's decision whether or not to call on your copywriting services. Your book will do some of the selling for you, but you have to do the rest.

What Samples Should I Include in My Portfolio?

Checklist 2 represents *ideal* materials you should include in your book. If you are fortunate enough to have more samples than you can squeeze into your portfolio, choose those that are the most successful (if measurable, quotable results are available), or that are the most *graphically* appealing (not necessarily the most well written). This may surprise you, but many potential clients will look at your samples, rather than read them, so it makes sense to show samples that look great.

If you are presenting your portfolio to a client, and you see him or her actually reading the materials, invite him or her to read a couple of your best sales letters. These are a faster read, and will best show your client how you can organize ideas in a strategic, compelling, and persuasive manner.

If your collection of samples is lacking in items from Checklist 2, consider including some items from Checklist 3.

When presenting your book, if your prospective client begins to look bored, stop. Don't show any more samples unless requested to do so. And never insist a client look at "just one more sample" — no matter how pertinent or impressive you may think it is.

Never discard a writing sample because you think it's not suitable for your portfolio. Keep everything you write. You never know when a client might have a nontraditional requirement — and your "unsuitable" sample becomes the best sample to show.

Checklist 2
IDEAL MATERIALS TO INCLUDE IN YOUR BOOK

❏ Print ads

❏ Sales letters

❏ Direct mail

❏ Mail-order packages exhibits

❏ Product or service descriptions

❏ Copy for trade show exhibits

❏ Trade show handouts

❏ Brochures

❏ Case studies and success stories

❏ Feature articles about products and services

❏ Media/press kits

❏ Press releases

❏ Annual reports

❏ Investor relations materials

❏ Product data sheets (often called "sell sheets")

❏ Flyers/circulars

❏ Packaging copy

❏ Any point-of-purchase (POP) and other product display copy

❏ Sales materials targeted at product resellers, distributors, and retailers (often called "alliance materials")

❏ Telemarketing scripts

❏ Product names, themes, slogans (referred to as "branding")

❏ CD-ROM and other scripted sales presentations

❏ Video scripts for products and services

❏ Fundraising letters and direct mail

❏ Promotional newsletters targeted at customers

❏ Internet direct mail (e-mail marketing messages)

❏ Internet banner ads

❏ Billboard ads

❏ Website content and copy

❏ Sales proposals

❏ Any other written collateral used in sales and marketing

Checklist 3
OTHER MATERIALS YOU CAN INCLUDE IN YOUR BOOK

☐ Business letters

☐ E-mail messages to customers and prospects

☐ Form letters and other templates

☐ Internal proposals

☐ Memos about new products and services

☐ Memos, letters, or e-mail written to seek project approval, gain consensus, or win others to your point of view

☐ Reports about new products and services

☐ Technical documentation about products

☐ Reports summarizing customer surveys

☐ Articles for internal newsletters and other publications

☐ Articles for external publications (especially business and trade magazines)

☐ Presentation notes, scripts, and storyboards (especially PowerPoint shows about new products and services)

☐ Seminar scripts, guides, and handouts (especially those targeted at customers, distributors, and resellers)

☐ Training materials (especially product education or sales training)

☐ Speeches

☐ User guides and electronic help menus

☐ Needs analysis

☐ Creative and project briefs

☐ Copy or editorial contributed to a website

☐ Sales or marketing documents written by others, but edited or rewritten by you

☐ Most other business documents, print and electronic

Collect a sample of everything you ever worked on. Even if you were not the primary copywriter, you may have contributed conceptual ideas to a project. (Just make sure you honestly indicate your contribution when you show the sample to a prospective client.)

Keep in mind that you don't necessarily have to have written the entire document to include the sample in your portfolio. If you have contributed a passage or two to a company brochure, annual report, proposal, website, or other business document, hang on to it. Just be sure to point out the specific areas you wrote when you show the piece to a prospect.

Collecting Samples of Your Work

If you have worked for an ad agency, you have an advantage when it comes to getting samples of your work. Agencies often keep for their own agency book dozens of samples of the work they have produced, so getting a few for yourself is rarely a problem. In fact, it's expected that you will retain at least one sample of any material you have contributed, even if you are leaving the agency.

If you worked for a corporation or smaller business and have helped write and produce ads or sales literature, getting samples is also not a problem. Did you contribute to the production of any sales literature? User guides? Ads? Or other forms of marketing communication? If so, collect a sample of each of these for your portfolio. Speeches, presentations, press releases, and feature articles are also important. And don't forget sales letters, proposals, customer service letters, and other documents you have written. Don't exclude anything. Take it all.

"But I've only written magazine articles. Should I include these in my book?" you might ask. Absolutely! In fact, I would also include the query letters you wrote to editors to get those article assignments. Query letters are, in fact, sales letters — which are great additions to any copywriter's portfolio.

"But My Client Won't Send Me Samples of My Work"

If you have already done some freelance writing for organizations, you have no doubt faced the frustrating task of getting clients to send you samples of produced work. I know many copywriters who actually include variations of the following clause in their quotations and agreements:

The client agrees to forward three copies of any work produced as a result, directly or indirectly, of my copywriting services on this project.

I have never used a clause like this as I worry that some clients might consider it bullying. Still, many copywriters do use it with degrees of success, so you might want to give this strategy a try.

Here's the reason it can sometimes be tough getting clients to send you samples: It takes time. And these days, time is a precious commodity. When you ask a client to mail you samples of your work, you're asking for a bigger favor than you may realize. It takes time to collect the samples, get an envelope, stamp it, address it, and send it to you. Clients will often say "Yes" to a request for samples — in fact, most are happy to do it — but more often than not, your request gets interminably buried near the bottom of their in-tray.

The best opportunity to get samples of your work is to ask for them in person at your next client meeting. If you're meeting to discuss a new project, its easy to end the meeting by saying, "By the way, Bob, do you have a spare copy of the direct-mail package I wrote for you last month? I'd love to include a copy in my portfolio." Most clients will say "Sure," and give you a copy then and there. If they say "No," or complain that their quantities are limited, ask for the next best thing: a laser-quality photocopy.

Of course, you may not have an opportunity to meet with your client for several weeks or months. I know many copywriters who rarely meet face-to-face with clients. Seattle-based high-tech copywriter Janice King says she sees her clients no more than once a year. Toronto copywriter Alan Sharpe says he has several clients he has never met. I'm in the same boat with many of my clients. So here's an approach I use to collect samples of my work.

Once I learn that a particular piece I wrote has been produced, I mail a letter (see Sample 3) to the client — and follow up two weeks later with an e-mail. The mailed letter includes an oversized, self-addressed, stamped envelope. This makes it easy for the client. All he or she has to do is grab a sample, stuff it in the envelope I provide, seal it, and toss it in the mail. (The two dollar stamp I include also adds an element of guilt. They think, "If he went to this much trouble to ask for a sample, the least I can do is send him one.")

Here's a trick that works well for me. These days, most design concepts are reviewed either online or as a PDF sent by e-mail. As the copywriter of the piece, ask if you can be on the review committee. Say that you would like to check that the text is laid out effectively and that everything works (which is a good idea for you to do anyway). This

"Make sure you get the job or docket number of any project you're working on," advises New York freelance copywriter Randy Rensch. "If your client is an ad agency or design firm, this makes it easier for them to pull some samples for you weeks or months later."

A PDF (Portable Document Format) is the standard in the design industry for sending clients concepts and updates for review. You can get a *free* "PDF Reader" at <www.adobe.com>.

Sample 3
LETTER FOR GETTING SAMPLES OF YOUR WORK FROM CLIENTS

The Marketing Group
99 Toronto Street, Suite 820
Buffalo, NY 88888

ATT: Tom McQuade

Hi Tom,

Thanks for asking me to contribute to your new Gizmo brochure. I understand it was recently printed and looks great. Congratulations.

Now I have a favor to ask. Can I get a copy of this brochure from you? It would be a great addition to my portfolio.

I've enclosed a stamped, self-addressed envelope for your convenience.

Thanks Tom,

Steve Slaunwhite
Steve Slaunwhite

way, you'll get an electronic version of the design in its final, or nearly final, form, with all the text in place. Just save it for your own portfolio.

Of course, there are times when, despite all your best efforts, a client simply will not send you a sample. There's not much you can do unless you want to be a pest. But there may be other ways to get samples of your work. I know a copywriter who got a friend to fill out a business reply card in a magazine, just to trick his client into sending him a copy of the brochure he wrote. (A little too mischievous for me, and I don't recommend it.) Another friend, in her efforts to get a copy of an ad she wrote years ago, actually photocopied it from microfilm in her local library. The only drawback was that the photocopy was grainy and in black and white.

Never Loan Your Original Samples

Guard your original samples with your life. If a prospective client asks you to send original samples of your work by mail (with the promise of returning them), send photocopies. If he or she insists that you mail originals, refuse.

If you give away your originals, and for some reason never get them back, it's a painful loss. There are many ways for a client to judge your capabilities without having to physically keep your samples. I sometimes send electronic samples of my work to clients by e-mail (using PDF files), which enables them to see my samples in full color. There is absolutely no reason for a client to request and keep originals.

I once met with a creative director who insisted that I leave my original samples with him "for a few days to show my colleagues and absorb the material." He went on to suggest that if I refused, then I was being unreasonable and we probably wouldn't be able to do business. I refused. We never did business. But I still have my samples. Never loan your original samples to anyone. Never.

"But I Don't Have Any Writing Samples"

I was recently asked, "If I don't have any copywriting samples, can I start a copywriting business?" The answer is, you can. It's going to be a little tougher at the beginning, but you can do it.

I once chatted with an ad agency executive who hired a freelance copywriter based solely on a flyer that the writer wrote for a garage sale. So it is possible to start in this business with very few samples to show.

If you show a prospect a customer service e-mail you have written, explain the strategy behind the e-mail. Why was it written? Who was the target market? How did you structure the e-mail to meet these objectives? What were the results? You get the idea.

But, first of all, are you sure you don't have any writing samples? It's difficult to get through life without writing something. Anything.

I suspect that if you take a close look at your background, you'll discover plenty of documents you have effectively written. They may not be ads, brochures, or direct mail, but you may have written a compelling customer service letter or a letter to the editor that was published in your local newspaper. Perhaps you have contributed a newsletter article for your professional association.

Take another look at Checklists 2 and 3 of potential portfolio samples for guidance. Chances are, you'll find you have one or two writing samples, however modest, to kick off your freelance copywriting efforts.

Clients are interested in seeing evidence — any evidence — that you have taken a writing task, however small, and conceptualized it, developed it, written it, and stuck with it through production. Even if it is just a letter.

If, after combing through everything you have written, you feel your portfolio is still lacking, consider these strategies for quickly generating more samples.

Volunteer writing for an association or charity

Do you belong to a professional association or club, or do you support a charity? If so, contribute articles to its newsletter (most associations publish a newsletter). Approach whomever is responsible for marketing, communications, or editorial. Tell him or her you are a writer and would love an opportunity to help out with any publications, flyers, brochures, websites, or member mailings the organization may be planning. Chances are, they will welcome the help. And you'll soon have more samples for your book.

Help a small-business owner

Small-business owners often do not have the budget to hire a professional copywriter for their advertising and marketing materials. Often, they write the copy themselves, spending what budget they do have on design and printing. Here is a great opportunity to volunteer your services. Contact the small-business owners you know locally. Explain to them that, for a limited time, you will be available at no charge to write any advertising and marketing materials they may be planning. Don't be humble in your approach. Simply point out that, like them, you are a small-business owner looking for ways to build your portfolio and reputation.

Help a freelance designer

Many freelance designers get requests from clients to do copywriting work — even though most designers hate to write copy or are not good at it. Here's where you can help. Contact some local independent designers in your area and tell them about your services. Explain that you are building your portfolio and may be able to do some copywriting work for them on a no-fee basis. They'll understand and respect your approach, and likely give you some work. Soon you will have a few samples to show.

Write for your employer

If you are currently working full time or part time, offer to do some writing tasks. An employee with strong writing skills is considered an important resource in most organizations. Tell your boss you're willing to help out with any letters, proposals, or reports he or she needs to produce. It can only make you look good.

I started this way. I offered to write sales brochures when I was a sales rep with a technology manufacturer. My goal at the time was a keen desire to improve the sales materials we used — not to collect samples for a portfolio. (I didn't even know then that I was destined to be a copywriter.) But this work did become an important part of my portfolio years later.

Write articles for small publications and e-zines

Local and regional newspapers, niche publications, and the surfeit of online publications and e-zines are often hungry for good contributing writers. These publications will pay very little, if anything, for articles, but this isn't the point. Articles, however short, can be a fine addition to your portfolio.

Contact the publication editor to outline your article suggestion and why you would be the perfect candidate to write it.

Take a course

The local community college in my city (Toronto) offers a course on copywriting. During the 12-week program, students work on a

If you're looking for business writing experience, your current job is a great place to start.

number of projects that they can eventually include in their portfolios.

Sometimes the projects are "live," which means they will actually be produced and used as marketing collateral. Author and sales coach Tom Stoyan recently told me his website was being produced by college students as a class project.

Contact the continuing education departments of local colleges and universities and ask if they offer copywriting courses.

Create spec samples

If you cannot get a copywriting assignment — even on a no-fee basis — then create your own copywriting job. Make up a fictional company with a fictional product and write a brochure, ad, press release, or any other marketing communications collateral that applies. This isn't as strange as it sounds. In the advertising community, this is called a "spec" piece. To break into this business, it is perfectly acceptable to demonstrate your creativity and writing skills with spec work.

This approach has the greatest chance of working with executives and creative directors of design firms and advertising agencies. Chances are, they had some spec pieces in their own portfolios earlier in their careers, so they are more inclined to give you a chance. Business managers and corporate executives, however, are less likely to respond well to this approach.

Get a job as a copywriter

I once watched a TV program about a young couple who decided to give up their corporate jobs to start a landscaping business. Instead of immediately hanging a shingle, they each spent an entire season working with local landscaping firms as general laborers. After a year of sweating, learning, and soaking up all the experience they could — earning not much more than minimum wage — they launched their own business. Today, they are highly successful and have a number of employees.

Sometimes I wish I had begun the same way, working as a writer at an ad agency or corporation before becoming self-employed. It might have made it easier for me to set up my own copywriting business.

Taking a course can be a great way to fill your portfolio (and learn more about copywriting).

If you don't have writing samples and experience in marketing, you might consider looking for work as a writer with an ad agency, design firm, public relations agency, investor relations agency, or major corporation. As a junior writer at an ad agency, you'll get a lot of the grunt work, often with many late nights and tight deadlines. But you'll learn. After a year or so, you'll have plenty of samples to show prospective clients. (And plenty of contacts in the industry.)

In the United States, you'll find copywriting opportunities in *Advertising Age, Business Marketing, Target Marketing, Direct Magazine,* and *Inside Direct Mail*. In Canada, look in *Marketing Magazine, Strategy,* and *Direct Marketing News*. The e-zine (online newsletter) *The Golden Thread* also advertises jobs for writers. You can subscribe for free at <www.awaionline.com/thegoldenthread>.

Try the sales letter idea

A friend of mine who had very few samples to show when he started as a freelance copywriter began with this great idea. He contacted local business owners and offered to write a sales letter for them at no charge. The only proviso was, if they liked the sales letter, they would agree to consider him for further copywriting assignments. Many business owners took him up on his offer. And soon, he had plenty of samples to show prospective clients. (This approach was so successful that, years later, he still uses this approach to promote his business.)

Don't forget your own marketing materials

Strange as it may seem, you don't always need samples of work you have completed for other clients to impress a current prospect. I often get assignments from new clients simply because they were impressed with the sales letter I sent them. (Sometimes they want me to write a sales letter just like it!) So write the most creative, dynamic sales letters, brochures, and other promotional materials you can for your own copywriting business. They may very well be the most important writing samples you show.

Putting It Together

Many copywriters keep their samples in large, black portfolio cases. These are familiar in advertising and design circles. However, I find them bulky and restricting, so I don't use one. Worse, they can be

If you want to get a job at an ad agency, start young. Agency executives don't like to admit it, but ageism does exist. It is very difficult to get a job as a junior copywriter past the age of 30.

Don't show a prospective client samples of your work until you have learned more about the client's needs. Once you have determined what these are, you can select appropriate samples to best sell yourself.

Most copywriters with online portfolios have them incorporated into their websites. You can view mine at <www.steveslaunwhite.com>. I also recommend Alan Sharpe's at <www.sharpecopy.com> and Donna Baier Stein's at <www.directcopy.com> as examples of portfolios that are impressively displayed, easy to view, and easy to read.

intimidating, especially for corporate or small-business clients. If you walk into a potential client's office with a large portfolio case, the client feels obligated to take the tour. In fact, many copywriters make the mistake of beginning a client meeting by showing off their portfolio of samples before knowing anything about the client.

When I attend a meeting with a potential client, I take a briefcase. Inside I include a series of small portfolio folders entitled Ads, Direct Mail, Brochures, Websites, and Case Studies. Once our meeting identifies the client's needs and project requirements, I can easily pull out the appropriate samples to support my argument that I'm the best copywriter for the job. Rarely do I show my entire portfolio. And I never show samples of my work before learning more about the client's needs.

When you do show a client samples of your work, remember that presentation counts. You can buy a plethora of folders and supplies that will help you create a clean, organized portfolio. There is absolutely no excuse for clumsily showing clients a series of loose, dog-eared samples.

A few years ago, I purchased a box of clear corner photo holders from a photography shop. I use these to mount my samples onto heavy paper, which I subsequently insert into the clear plastic linings of my portfolio folders. The effect looks very professional, my samples stay crisp and presentable for years, and I am able to easily pull out samples during a meeting if the client wants a closer look.

As the saying goes: You never get a second chance to make a first impression.

Creating an Online Portfolio

These days, almost all your clients will have access to the Internet, and an increasing number will have a continuous, high-speed connection. This is especially true if your client works for a large ad agency or corporation. Today, clients are relying more and more on the Internet to find, research, and select vendor services. And this includes copywriting services.

If you don't already have an online portfolio, I suggest you put one together soon. Today, it's an advantage. Tomorrow, it will be a necessity.

Why have an online portfolio?

There are several advantages to creating an online portfolio:

- *It makes a great marketing tool.* You can use your online portfolio in tandem with other marketing promotions, such as advertisements and direct mail. For example, I use a postcard mailing to invite potential clients to review my online portfolio.

- *You can use it for inquiry fulfillment.* When clients call to ask for information about your services, you can direct them to your website. This makes inquiry fulfillment quicker, and may get you an order sooner. It also helps to head off requests for a live meeting to review your book, which can be a time-consuming task.

- *It makes it easier to get assignments by phone.* In the past, when a client called with a potential project and wanted to see samples of my work, I would have to arrange a live meeting or mail photocopy samples. With an online portfolio, I can now direct a prospective client to my samples while I still have him or her on the phone. This gives me the opportunity to answer questions and discuss the project — and often get the order before I hang up the phone. An online portfolio dramatically shortens the sales process and helps to secure more assignments, sooner.

- *It instantly makes your business global.* The Internet is a global marketplace. When you have your portfolio online, you are exposing your business to an international market. Potential clients from other states or provinces and from around the world can view your portfolio and e-mail or call with inquiries about your services. Many copywriters have reported that the perceived geographical boundaries of their business vanished soon after launching their websites and online portfolios.

There are also some drawbacks to an online portfolio:

- *It costs time and money.* Securing a domain name, signing on with a web hosting service, designing a website, scanning your portfolio for viewing on the Internet, and keeping your online portfolio up-to-date adds an upfront and continuous cost to your copywriting business.

A domain name is an address on the Internet. For example, copywriter Joe Vitale's domain name is <mrfire.com> so his Internet address is <www.mrfire.com>.

If you plan to secure a domain name for your copywriting business, do it sooner rather than later. To learn more about reserving your own Internet domain name, visit <www.NetworkSolutions.com>.

- *You lose some control.* With your physical book of samples, you can select exactly which ads, brochures, and other marketing materials you want to show a potential client based on his or her specific project requirements. This puts you in control of the selling process. When your portfolio is online, however, you have no say in who sees your samples, and which samples they choose to view and read.

Putting together your online portfolio

Is an online portfolio difficult to create? Actually it's quite easy. Here are some things you'll need to know to create yours:

Get a website address

The first step in "getting online" is to reserve a domain name. This is the name that becomes part of your web address … the address that's typed into your Internet browser to get to your website. My domain name is SteveSlaunwhite.com, so my web address is <www.steveslaunwhite.com>.

When I first reserved the domain name for my website, it cost about $100 plus a hefty yearly fee. That was many years ago. Today, because of competition among Internet service providers, domain name registration doesn't cost much more than a large café latte. As of this writing, GoDaddy.com, one of many companies that register domain names, charges less than $10.

The advantage of having your own domain name is that it's yours forever (as long as you keep paying your annual fee). It makes you look more professional and less fly-by-night. I find that more and more potential clients I talk to ask, "So what's your website address?" Can you imagine how antiquated I'd feel if I didn't have one!

Sign up with a web hosting service

To get your portfolio on the Internet, you'll need to register with a web hosting service. These services store your website on their servers and make your site accessible to others on the Internet. They charge a monthly fee ranging from $15 to $75 depending on the type of hosting services you require. Because your online portfolio will contain graphics, tell your web hosting service you need at least 20 megabits (megs) of space. There are plenty of web hosting services available. I'm very happy with mine: <www.netnation.com>.

Decide which portfolio samples to include

When you put together a book of printed samples, it's simple. You can choose to include or not include any samples you wish. You can shuffle them around and present them anyway you like. It's easy to have dozens of samples representing a variety of project types in your physical portfolio. This isn't so for an online portfolio. You have to be selective, because having dozens of samples on your website isn't practical. It can be difficult to maintain and for clients to browse. So you have to choose carefully.

Most copywriters divide their online portfolios into categories, such as advertising, direct mail, brochures, websites, e-mail, case studies, and annual reports. This makes it easier for clients to find and view those samples that pertain specifically to their project requirements. If you decide to take this approach, include two or three of your best samples under each category.

Choose the samples from your book that have high brand recognition (e.g., IBM, Mattel, Kellogg's), represent your best work, are visually appealing, and are typical (i.e., not unusual projects to which most clients will not relate).

Convert your portfolio to online images

If a professional designer or Internet development professional is creating your website and online portfolio, then converting your portfolio to online images is easy. Just select the samples you want online and hand them over. They'll do the rest.

But if you're creating your online portfolio yourself, you'll have to scan your samples and convert them into graphic files suitable for display on the Internet. Most web page construction software (e.g., Microsoft FrontPage or DreamWeaver) can import graphic files in various formats. For more information on creating a website and online portfolio, take a look at *Writing for the Web: Geeks' Edition*, another title published by Self-Counsel Press.

Decide how your online samples will be read

Obviously, as a copywriter, many potential clients will want to read your samples, not just look at them. It's important to make this task as easy as possible for the viewer. Remember, no one wants to read text by squinting at a computer screen.

Some online portfolios contain a link to a larger image of the sample so you can read the text. This allows viewers to read the copy in context with the layout and visuals. However, downloading large graphic files can be sluggish, and some clients won't wait.

Another option is to have a separate text file available for those who want to read the copy. For example, you could have a dazzling image of the piece in all its glory, with a "Read Me" link beside it. If a potential client wants to read the text, he or she simply clicks the link and the copy is displayed in an easy-to-read format.

Lately, many copywriters have been including PDF links to portfolio samples. These are flexible in that a potential client can easily view the image, enlarge it to read the text, and even save it for further reference. PDF portfolio samples are also handy when a prospect or client wants you to send samples by e-mail.

Get the word out

Launching an online portfolio is another great excuse for promoting your copywriting services. It's news. So send announcements to current clients, and those who have recently inquired about your services. A postcard notification works well, as does an e-mail containing a hot link to your new online presence.

Keep it up-to-date

The Internet is a culture of "new." Don't allow your online portfolio to grow old and stale. When you've completed an exciting new project, include the work in your portfolio. Place a "new" sign next to it to allow repeat visitors to your site to immediately recognize the content as new.

5
Identifying Target Markets

Are you ready to find some clients for your copywriting business? If you're at this stage, you are no doubt excited to get moving toward establishing yourself as a self-employed professional. Perhaps you're ready to pepper local business publications with advertisements? Publish your website? Litter the market with sales letters and other mailings? My advice to you is to slow down (just a little).

I don't want to dampen your initial enthusiasm, but I have seen many self-employed professionals begin with expensive campaigns for new clients without really knowing — and, more important, *understanding* — who their prospects are. I've witnessed many people who, rather than take the time to clearly define their markets, cast a big net, hoping to catch any business. They go on spending sprees with mass mailings and ads aimed at poor prospects — usually with unhappy results.

Before you begin your marketing campaign, decide on your target market. Will you focus on the agency side or the client side? Are there certain industries you have intimate knowledge of? Do your homework and you won't waste effort and money on poor prospects.

You need to clearly identify your target markets before you begin a marketing effort. The more you understand about the people to whom you are selling your services, the greater your results will be. For example, are you going to focus on the agency side or the client side? (See more on this later in this chapter.) Which industries are you going to focus on? Technology? Finance? Consumer goods? All sectors? How about size? Are you going to market to large Fortune 500 corporations, or small, entrepreneurial start-ups? And, within those companies, to whom will you market? Sales managers? Marketing managers? Creative directors? Owners? What are their potential motives for hiring your copywriting services? Are they looking for a great portfolio? Fast project turnaround? Or both? What marketing problems do they face that you could potentially solve?

Create the clearest picture you can of your target markets and the individuals in those markets most likely to hire your services, and your marketing efforts will be off to a great start.

Start with What Brought You Here

Years ago, I attended a seminar called "Making the Transition to Self-Employment." A young woman in the audience raised her hand and asked, "How do I decide what type of business to get into?" The seminar speaker answered, "Start with what brought you here." That's good advice for deciding what types of clients you are going to approach. If you want to find clients for your copywriting business sooner (rather than later), you need to target those prospects that best fit with your background and experience.

Your background — educational, professional, even personal — is your uniqueness and your advantage in getting copywriting clients.

Before becoming a full-time copywriter, my background was in technical sales, so I began writing sales brochures and other collateral for technical products. This wasn't necessarily what I wanted to do with my copywriting practice — what I really wanted to do was write direct mail — but it was a great place to start. I found clients much more quickly than I would have if I had presented myself as a direct-mail copywriter (with no experience). It was a stepping stone, and today half my business is writing successful direct mail.

I suggest you adopt a similar strategy. For example, if you have an ad agency background in software products, you have an excellent chance of attracting the attention of creative directors at *other* ad agencies who handle software clients. (In fact, you probably know many of them.) So don't toss this advantage in the trash just because you're tired of software and want to try health-care marketing. Start with software. Once your copywriting business is a going concern, you'll find it much easier to laterally expand into other areas of interest.

Take a close look at what brought you to the copywriting business. Where have you worked? At a design firm? The marketing department of a major insurance company? On a farm? (Remember, former farm girl Brenda Kruse now thrives writing copy for agri-businesses.) Leverage your background, your experience, your contacts. If you have a pharmaceutical background, for example, don't look for clients in the magazine publishing industry (at least, not yet). Start by offering your services to marketing managers of pharmaceutical firms. This is a huge and very lucrative market that many copywriters don't have the expertise to serve. You do.

"But I'm tired of banking (or the automotive industry, or investor relations)," you might say. "I want to try something different." I can certainly understand wanting to make a complete right turn in your life and venturing off into an entirely new field. And maybe you *should* try a completely different focus, especially if you're burnt out or sick of the industry you're in. But you will attract more clients more easily if you target the markets in which you have the most experience.

Agency Side or Client Side

On the broadest level, the market for copywriting services is divided into two very distinct groups: the agency side and the client side.

The agency side is advertising agencies, design firms, public relations agencies, marketing consultants, investor relations agencies — any firm that handles creative work and/or production on behalf of their clients. For example, Ogilvy & Mather is an agency that produces print ads and develops advertising campaigns for their many corporate clients. For these services they are paid a fee, or commission, for both. If Ogilvy & Mather calls on your copywriting services, you will be working under their supervision on a project for their client. When you submit your invoice, you get paid by Ogilvy & Mather, not by their client.

The client side involves those businesses and organizations that are asking for the materials to actually be produced — ads, brochures, websites, any printed or electronic collateral they may need. Instead of going through their agency or design firm, they are hiring you directly to write the copy. Often, this will involve working in tandem with their in-house designer, design firm, or agency. If Microsoft calls on you to write a sales letter for a new software product, for example, they would be a client on the client side. (Among freelance creatives, the client side is also referred to as "working direct.")

Most self-employed copywriters I have spoken with have clients on both the agency side and the client side. Many deal exclusively with agencies. A few deal only with direct clients. My current mix is 50-50, but since I prefer to work with direct corporate clients, my client mix is rapidly shifting toward the client side.

Which side should you target? If you come from an agency background, you will likely have better luck attracting ad agency clients. If you're a former marketing manager in the telecommunications industry, however, you might consider working directly with telecommunications companies (or positioning yourself with agencies and design firms as a telecommunications/copywriting expert).

Table 1 provides a comparison of agency side versus client side that might prove helpful in determining where to focus your marketing efforts.

The Top Markets for Copywriting Services

Some industry sectors are proven fertile ground for attracting clients and growing your copywriting business. The best of these are listed below. While virtually all businesses and organizations can use your copywriting services, the list represents those businesses that most often seek out and hire freelance copywriters on an ongoing basis.

Advertising agencies

You may wonder why an advertising agency would need your copywriting services. After all, don't they have their own staff of writers? The answer is: some do; a lot don't.

Table 1
COMPARISON OF AGENCY SIDE VERSUS CLIENT SIDE

AGENCY SIDE	CLIENT SIDE
Markets	
A proven market for freelance copywriters. Just about every agency uses outside copywriting services from time to time. When you sell copywriting to an agency, you're selling to the converted.	For smaller businesses your copywriting services may be a hard sell in terms of demonstrating value and getting your price. Larger corporations are a proven market, yet some may prefer to deal exclusively with ad agencies and design firms — not freelancers.
Contacts	
Ad agencies and design firms are easily identified. You'll have little difficulty finding a list or directory with the names of owners and creative directors — your key prospects.	Finding good business and contact information on direct clients is more difficult. You'll have to dig deeper to come up with the names of qualified prospects, and this increases your time and costs of marketing.
Budgets	
Your copywriting service is a sub-contracted or "pass through" expense. They will mark up your fee on their invoice to their client. This means you can expect to get 20 percent to 30 percent less from an agency client than you normally would from a direct corporate client.	Direct clients, especially larger corporations, have the budget to pay more. Since you are billing direct, there is no intermediary — such as an ad agency — to mark up your fees. You can expect to receive 20 percent to 30 percent more for your work than you would from an ad agency or design firm.
Demands	
Agencies will find the clients, make the deals, handle most of the client contact for you, brief you on each project, and supply you with the background materials you need. All you do is write the copy.	Direct clients will demand more from you. You may have to attend numerous meetings, coordinate your activities with their designer or agency, and become more involved in concepts and strategy. You are as much a consultant as you are a copywriter.

Table 1 — Continued

AGENCY SIDE	CLIENT SIDE

Presentation

Agencies are great at presentation. Once you write a copy draft, the agency will present it to the client for you, brought to life with sharp visuals, graphics, and other design elements.

As a freelance copywriter you don't have an art department. You can present your copy only in draft form — with no visuals or design. This is fine for most clients, but some may have difficulty visualizing your copy in context with the finished product.

Deadlines

Deadlines tend to be tight. This is because an agency or design firm needs time to receive your copy, lay it out with their design and visuals, and present it to their client. They will ask for your copy as soon as possible, sometimes dictating next-to-impossible deadlines.

In my experience, deadlines are twice as long for direct clients as compared to the agency side. They can still be tight, but you have much more elbow room.

Payment

Some agencies and design firms, especially smaller ones, can be slow to pay your invoices. Like any small business, they are vulnerable to cash-flow crunches. And freelancers tend to be at the end of the feeding trough in terms of who gets paid first.

Direct corporate clients usually pay very well. In most cases, your legitimate invoice to a major corporation is almost as good as money in the bank. But you still have to be careful with small- and mid-sized businesses.

Variety

Because most ad agencies deal with multiple clients and juggle multiple projects, they can offer you a variety of work from different industries. You may be asked to write a sales letter for their banking client one week, then be tasked with writing a website for their automotive client the next.

When you work with a direct client, you write about their products and services only. The projects themselves may vary — a print ad one month, a direct-mail package the next — but the content rarely changes. You might get bored. Or, like me, you might enjoy becoming a long-standing expert on your client's product and service offerings.

Larger ad agencies (those with 25 or more employees) usually have at least one writer on staff. These writers handle the day-to-day copy tasks — press releases, packaging copy, brochures, taglines, slogans, and blurbs for trade-show displays. In many agencies, the copywriter and the art director make up a creative team, and together they build their reputation working on major campaigns. It's not uncommon for a highly successful creative team to move from one agency to another, chasing better money and more prestigious clients. Some creative teams go on to launch their own businesses.

So why would an ad agency with a cadre of writers need your copywriting services? Ad agencies suffer from an ebb and flow of work, and often get very busy at unpredictable times. So, one day, the agency writers are yawning and creating origami at their desks; the next, they're ordering pizza and working evenings and weekends on a new ad campaign for a major new client. This is when ad agencies need to call on outside writers to handle the overload.

This is good news for your business because a large agency can give you a lot of overflow work. Unfortunately, these types of assignments often come with tight deadlines, which can be stressful. I recently received a call from an agency asking if I could write a press release for them by 11:00 a.m. that day. And it was already 9:30 a.m.! (I politely turned them down.)

An agency with staff writers may also call on your services for specialized work. You may have experience with a particular type of project, product, or industry that their in-house writers can't handle. This could include projects such as video scripts, annual reports, and e-commerce websites, or products that require technical knowledge such as industrial photo imaging or investment derivatives. Agency staff writers often don't have the time (or inclination) to develop the expertise needed to successfully complete such projects. So they call you.

While there are many ad agencies that employ staff writers, there are many more that don't. Most small- to mid-sized agencies — and especially design firms — do not have a copywriter on staff. They *routinely* send out work to freelancers. And there are many more smaller agencies and design firms than large ad agencies. Obviously, these firms tend to be a great market for freelance copywriters.

Many large ad agencies will need your services to fill in for sick days, vacations, maternity leaves, and resignations. Last year, I did some work for a major direct marketing agency because of summer vacations.

Who are the best people to contact at an ad agency or a design firm for freelance copywriting work? I have found it best to start with the creative director and, in smaller firms, the owner. (In fact, sometimes the owner and the creative director are the same person.)

Don't forget agency hybrids: those companies that do work similar to ad agencies but more specialized.

For example, public relations (PR) agencies primarily handle publicity and media relations. Like ad agencies, they produce a mountain of print and online communications on behalf of their clients — brochures, press releases, backgrounders, websites, Video News Releases (VNRS), and more. Some also handle speechwriting for executives.

PR agencies use freelance copywriters for much the same reason as ad agencies do. They become overworked and need outside help. Or they require specialized expertise that they don't have in-house, such as direct-mail copywriting.

There's another class of agencies that I've done a lot of work for, and that's Investor Relations (IR) agencies. These firms specialize in investor, shareholder, and financial communications — primarily for publicly traded companies. They routinely produce news releases, quarterly reports, backgrounders, Q&A's, presentations, brochures, and more in their quest to promote (or explain away) the financial condition of their client's company. These are all potentially well-paying assignments for freelance copywriters. But I've found that the best project an IR agency can hand you is the coveted annual report.

An annual report is typically a big, glossy brochure — sometimes as big as a book — that contains promotional information on the company along with audited financial statements. As a copywriter, you'll have nothing to do with the financial statements. That's the auditing firm's job. Your job will be to write the pages about the company's products, management team, philosophy, work in the community, and so forth.

Annual reports are big business for many copywriters. You can expect to earn between $5,000 and $10,000 per project! And since the shelf life of these documents is only twelve months, it's a job that can renew itself year after year.

The best person to contact? Try the president or the manager of client relations.

Corporations

Large corporations — those with 100 or more front office employees — are a big market for freelance copywriters. The marketing division of a single corporation, for example, can produce scores of direct mailings, ads, brochures, case studies, media packages, new product releases, promotional newsletters, websites, and other printed and electronic collateral each year, a small portion of which can keep you very busy.

Most of my corporate work comes from the marketing department, but other departments within a corporation will also use your copywriting savvy from time to time. The public relations department may want you to write press releases and media kits. The sales department could assign you the task of rewriting model sales letters (an assignment I recently completed for one of my corporate clients). The investor relations department may call you in to write the corporate annual report (which can be a very lucrative project).

How much work can a corporation give you? One of my Fortune 500 clients currently represents 25 percent of my business. And I don't have *all* their business. Most of their business, in fact, goes to their ad agency, which handles branding and ad campaigns. They call on me for direct mail, sales letters, and special projects involving sales brochures and other collateral.

Who are the best people to approach at a corporation for copywriting assignments? In my experience, marketing managers are the best prospects for corporate copywriting work. Their job is to get the sales message out. This means coordinating with ad agencies, design firms, and freelance copywriters in a nonstop effort to produce marketing communications that distinguish their products and services in the marketplace.

Besides marketing managers, you should also look for titles such as product manager, marketing communications manager, advertising manager, communications manager, and new business development manager.

Direct Marketers

Take a look at your mail or e-mail inbox. Every day you receive promotions from companies wanting you to subscribe to a magazine, buy a collectable, join a book club, change your long-distance plan,

"There are lots of opportunities for copywriters in the nonprofit sector, [including] membership mailings, fundraising appeal mailings, and renewal mailings. Copy is much more important than design in nonprofit mail."

— Donna Baier Stein, a top direct-mail specialist and author of a great book on copywriting called *Write on Target*.

order a series of cookbooks, travel to a resort — it never ends. The derogatory term for this is junk mail. But you might want to use another word to describe it: opportunity.

Some of the most famous, highly paid copywriters in the world have built their reputations in the direct marketing industry. Each year hundreds of millions of direct-mail packages — and online promotions, too — are sent out into the world. Some do very well; others don't. The thinking in the industry is that the copy is the key differentiator between a successful promotion and a loser. That's why direct marketers are willing to pay very well for effectively written copy.

Just about every kind of organization uses direct marketing to some extent. But the most common are charities, advocacy groups, companies that market software, automotive goods, credit cards, collectibles, home study courses, audio/visual programs, insurance services, telecommunications services, travel opportunities, newsletters, and magazines.

When a direct marketer asks you to write a package, you'll be writing a direct-mail or e-mail piece that does all the selling … gaining attention, introducing the product, motivating the buyer, and getting the order. It's not easy. But the good news is, there are plenty of books, courses, and other resources that will show you how. (See the Resources section on the CD-ROM included with this book.)

Who do you contact? Your potential client will have a title such as marketing manager or direct marketing manager.

Charities and other nonprofit organizations

Nonprofits are organizations that, as the name implies, are specifically set up not to make a profit. But that doesn't mean they don't have money to spend!

Charities, advocacy groups, churches, membership organizations, and trade associations all fall under the nonprofit banner.

The types of copywriting assignments that a nonprofit can hire you for are similar to those of a corporate client. However, writing fundraising letters and direct-mail packages is by far the most lucrative. Why? Because fundraising is the lifeblood of nearly every nonprofit organization. You have no doubt received fundraising appeals

"Don't be fooled into thinking it is easier to break into the small-business market," says Diana Wimbs in her book Freelance Copywriting. "They tend to operate on much tighter budgets and will want some pretty tough arguments … to convince them of your value."

from numerous charities in your mail. (If you haven't, just donate a few dollars to a charity and see what happens.)

In most jurisdictions, however, charities are restricted as to how much they can spend raising funds. (This is usually set as a maximum percentage of funds received.) So the amount you can charge a charity is usually less than what you could receive from a corporate client — anywhere from half to two-thirds your normal corporate rate. But this doesn't make the nonprofit sector a poor market.

Fundraising letters and packages, the type of assignments charities most often farm out to freelance copywriters, use a fairly standardized format. This is usually a two- to four-page letter, sometimes including a small brochure or other insert. Once you've written a few, you can write them faster than you could a similar-sized direct-mail package selling products or services. And a single national charity can provide you with several fundraising letters and packages to write each year.

Some ad agencies and design firms — and even some copywriters (myself included) — offer their creative services to favored charities for low or no fees. In the industry, this is called *pro bono*. There are, however, plenty of freelance copywriters who make an excellent living — and perhaps feel an altruistic sense of goodwill — writing fundraising appeals for charities and other nonprofit organizations.

The best person to contact at a charity is the fundraising director.

Professional associations

Although not actually charities, most professional associations are also not-for-profit organizations. There are many around. In fact, there is probably an association for every group of professions, interests, backgrounds, and goals imaginable. (There is even an association for associations!)

National associations often hire copywriters to create ads, sales letters, and direct-mail campaigns that attract new members or get existing members to renew their memberships. Expect to be paid at or near your corporate rate — many national associations are very financially well-off. At a recent meeting of an association I'm involved in, the president proudly announced we now had a two-year operating reserve in the bank. Not too many businesses can boast that.

Essentially a marketing document, a corporate annual report can be a lucrative assignment for a copywriter. As Maryclaire Collins points out in her book *How to Make Money Writing Corporate Communications*, "Many companies rely on the same annual report writers for years and pay them munificently for their services."

The best person to contact for copywriting work at an association is the membership director.

Less Likely Markets — but Still Prospects

Small businesses

I've worked with a number of small-business clients over the years, with mixed results. There are a number of obstacles you will need to overcome in order to succeed in this market:

- *Price sensitivity.* Small-business marketing budgets tend to be small. Chances are, small-business owners will balk at your corporate rates and want to haggle. This is especially true for very small businesses where your fees are essentially coming out of the business owner's pocket. They'll want you to justify every dollar. (As a small-business owner myself, I find it hard to blame them.)

- *Inexperience in dealing with copywriters.* While a corporate marketing manager or ad agency pro will have plenty of experience with designers and copywriters, small-business owners tend to be less savvy. This is probably because a small-business owner has to wear so many hats — manager, accountant, product developer, salesperson, marketer, and creative producer. In fact, he or she may have never worked with a copywriter before and may be unfamiliar with the process or even with what it is that a copywriter does.

I once wrote an annual report for a very small resource company. It was the first time they had used a copywriter. In a draft of the report I sent them, I casually suggested they include a graph of their five-year sales summary. A few weeks later my client called me and said, "Steve, we're ready to go to print. Where's the design of that five-year sales summary you promised us?"

The lesson? When dealing with small-business owners, always clarify exactly what you will be delivering. One way of doing this is to write in your quotation —

> *I will deliver the text of your brochure on computer disk or hard copy — your choice. My copywriting services do not include formatting graphs, tables, or any layout or design work of any kind.*

- *Looking for the whole package.* Small businesses tend to look for turnkey solutions to their marketing problems. So to them, hiring your copywriting services may seem like trying to clap with one hand. Who is going to handle the design? Photography? Illustrations? Printing? You can somewhat eliminate this obstacle by building a network of self-employed designers, photographers, and illustrators to whom you can refer your clients. On copywriter Bob Bly's website, <www.bly.com>, he maintains a list of preferred vendors. When someone calls Bob for a direct-mail package and asks about design, he refers his client to the Direct Mail Designers section of his Preferred Vendors page. I recommend that you, too, cultivate a network of preferred vendors, especially if you target smaller businesses (and even if you focus on major corporate accounts).

The upside of targeting the small-business market is that it is large. More than 80 percent of the businesses in North America have fewer than 50 employees. And there are hundreds of small-business start-ups every day — all needing brochures, ads, websites, and other marketing materials.

If you intend to target the small-business market, aim your efforts directly at the owner. In my experience with small businesses, it's a waste of time to talk to anyone else.

Governments

I don't have much experience selling copywriting services to government departments and agencies, but I know that government business can provide steady work for those who specialize in it. In federal government centers such as Washington and Ottawa, there are entire firms of writers dedicated exclusively to government work.

Most writing assignments offered by government bodies tend to be informational in nature. These are communications written to inform and explain — not to sell. But governments certainly also produce ads, direct mail, and marketing communications.

There is one major drawback to government clients. Most of the copywriters I know who target this market complain of the arduous procurement process. Even for smaller projects, there often is a plethora of red tape — forms, authorizations, waivers, quotations, and requests for quotation — before you receive your purchase order.

Each government department has its own procurement process. I suggest you begin by targeting the communications manager, marketing manager, or marketing communications manager of each department.

6
How to Get Clients

Here's a question. To succeed as a freelance copywriter, which is the most important skill for you to develop: learning to write great copy, or learning to attract great clients?

Of course, both are important. Crucial, in fact. But if you must err on one side, I suggest you focus on cultivating your ability to find and retain clients. Hone this skill to a sharp edge, and you can overcome virtually any other obstacle in your business. After all, if you have no clients, you have no business.

Think about it. Does it matter how gifted a copywriter you are if you can't find clients? I've known many talented people who were unable to make a go of it as a self-employed "whatever" simply because they couldn't — or stubbornly wouldn't — improve their sales and self-promotion skills. Don't be one of those people. Your ability to consistently find clients for your copywriting business is your best insurance against slow times and a plummeting bank account.

There are three plans you'll have to make in order to attract new clients — quickly and consistently — for your copywriting business:

1. Prospecting plan

2. Fulfillment plan

3. Keep-in-touch plan

Creating a Successful Prospecting Plan

A lot of people are confused, and even a little intimidated, by the word prospecting. Some don't understand what prospecting is, and have no idea what's involved in approaching prospective clients. Others envision an aggressive, get-your-foot-in-the-door sales tactic — one that's filled with one rejection after another, leaving you emotionally battered and bruised.

Let's clear the air.

Prospecting is really quite simple. It is the process of telling folks what you do, how they benefit, and what they need to know to hire your services. That's it. Not much of a mystery here, is there?

Consider one of the target markets you have identified in Chapter 5. Let's say it is local advertising agencies. Does everyone in those agencies — the account executives, the creative directors, the owners — know who you are, and that you provide copywriting services? Probably not. In fact, you may be missing out on assignments simply because potential clients don't know you exist.

So tell them! That's the essence of prospecting. It's simple. But it works.

I know many freelance professionals who have built an enviable list of lucrative clients just by telling people — lots and lots of people — exactly what it is they do.

One of the most successful copywriters I know is my friend Ivan Levison. (For more information about him, read Chapter 12.) The first five words on his website are: "Hi. I'm a freelance copywriter ..." He leaves visitors with no doubt as to the service he provides.

So how do you tell lots and lots of people what *you* do? The options are virtually limitless, as you'll discover later in this chapter. I prefer a combination of letters, calls, and articles. You may want to schmooze at conferences and place ads in the trades. How you do it is not the most important thing. Doing it is.

While it's true that you can get by quite nicely simply by telling lots of folks what you do, if you want to crank it up a notch — so you can get more and better clients, faster — you also need to tell people how you help. To put it in familiar copywriting lingo, you need to bring in a benefit or two.

On my website, for example, I tell potential clients that I'm a copywriter. (Prospecting Principle 1: Tell 'em what you do.) But I follow up quickly with a list of three specific benefits that my services provide. (Prospecting Principle 2: Tell 'em how you help.) Clients have said many times that it was these "how I help" bullets that first prompted them to call me.

The third prospecting principle is to tell people what they need to know to hire your services. This may seem ridiculously self-evident. After all, shouldn't potential clients know that all they have to do is pick up the phone and hire your services? Not necessarily. I'm constantly surprised, when I review marketing materials from other copywriters, by the lack of phone numbers, e-mail addresses, and other basic contact information. There are countless copywriter websites, for example, that don't have phone numbers or postal addresses! As a potential client, you're forced to send an e-mail and hope for the best. In some cases, you can't even do that. One copywriter website I visited recently required all potential clients to submit an online contact form. No alternative means of reaching the writer was provided. Guess what? The online submit form didn't work. Do you think a prospect would wait and try again later? Not a chance.

You need to make it easy for people to reach you. There's absolutely no reason why you should put up obstacles. If you don't want to publish a phone number — perhaps because it's your personal home number — then get a second line. Preferably a business line.

In addition to basic contact information, you also need to address the questions all prospects have before they call: "How do I get a quote?" "How do I hire your services?" "Can we do it over the phone, or do we need a meeting?"

The three prospecting principles:

1. Tell them what you do.
2. Tell them how they benefit.
3. Tell them how to hire your services.

"You have the writing and communication skills, so use them to your advantage in letters," advises Diana Wimbs in her book *Freelance Copywriting*. "Even if companies and agencies are not looking for freelance copywriters at the time, they will usually keep interesting approaches on file for future reference."

Sales letters don't require extensive design work — in fact, they can easily be created on your own letterhead. Your main cost is postage.

Again, these may seem obvious — to you. But not necessarily to prospective clients. Why leave anything to chance? In my prospecting materials, and on my website, I make it clear that anyone can call me to discuss a project and receive a prompt quotation on their specific requirements. I include all my contact details: phone, fax, postal address, and e-mail.

So, now that we've taken some of the mystery out of prospecting, let's take a closer look at the various methods of reaching out to potential clients.

Sales letters

Despite the proliferation of e-mail, good old-fashioned letters mailed through the post office — sales letters, as they are most commonly known — are one of the most effective means of reaching prospects. They are simple to use. You can rewrite or update them anytime, without the extra costs associated with redoing ads or brochures. And, once they're in the mail, they work on their own while you do other things. It's like having your own little army of sales people in the field pitching your services.

When I began my copywriting practice, I used sales letters extensively. I still do. They are the workhorses of my prospecting machine. Some of my best clients, those that have given me tens of thousands of dollars, and in a couple of cases, hundreds of thousands of dollars in business over the years came as a result of a sales letter. It's worth the price of a stamp!

Here's how it works:

Let's say you write a one-page sales letter targeting creative directors at direct marketing agencies. You send out 100 letters and receive one response (a call, an e-mail, a fax.) Then you send out 100 more sales letters and you receive another response. You've done it! You have created a prospecting machine that generates a one percent response rate. Now you can mail your letters with confidence, knowing that you will average one reply for every 100 letters you send out.

"But one percent doesn't seem like much," you might be saying. Rest assured, it is.

The great thing about this business is that you don't need that many clients to fill your schedule with lucrative writing assignments. Some copywriters do very well with less than ten! So if you mail 500 letters, and get 5 responses, you'll likely be able to convert one or two of those five into new clients. Now you're in business!

Sales letters are very flexible and cost effective. Depending on how busy I am, I can simply call my assistant and say, "Send out 300 letters to list B." Then I can get back to work, knowing my little paper army is out there, selling for me.

How do you write a sales letter that generates a one percent response rate or more?

Here is a format that is proven to work well:

- Gain attention with a captivating headline

- Highlight a problem the prospect may be having (e.g., "Is your website copy closing enough sales?")

- Position your services as the solution

- Provide evidence of your qualifications (clients, testimonials, awards, track records, experience, etc.)

- Make them an offer (e.g., "Call or e-mail to request samples of my work.")

Chances are, most interested prospects who receive your letter will not have an assignment available for you right away. So you need to make them an offer that keeps you on the radar screen. I have found that offering to send an "Information Kit" of some kind works extremely well. Later, in the section "Creating an Effective Fulfillment Plan," I'll show you what to include in an information package to prospective clients.

Want to hear an inside tip that is guaranteed to double the response to your sales letter? In the P.S. statement, sweeten the deal by offering a "how-to" report or article of some kind. For example, you could say:

P.S. When you e-mail for your free Information Kit, don't forget to ask for a free copy of my recent article: "7 Tips for Writing Landing Pages That Sell."

"Self-mailers [including postcards] eliminate the envelope barrier and start selling immediately," says Sandra Blum in her book *Designing Direct Mail That Sells.* "Self-mailers tend to get past gatekeepers and get delivered in businesses, probably because they are pretty nonthreatening."

A cost-saving tip: Check with your local post office for special rates for mass postcard mailings.

In direct marketing, this technique is called an information premium. It works well for two reasons. First, it gives a potential client another great reason to reply to your letter. Second, the article, report or guide that you offer positions you as an expert.

For years I offered a professionally published e-book called *101 Writing Tips for Successful E-mail Marketing* in my sales letters. Not only did this boost the response to my mailings, it also motivated clients to hire me to write their e-mail promotions! Even today, e-mail marketing represents almost one-third of my business!

I suggest you write, test, rewrite, and improve your sales letter until you achieve at least a one percent response. If you can get more than that, great. All my letters pull a 2 to 4 percent response. Some have even generated up to a 7 percent response, but those are rarer. See Sample 4 for one of my lead-generating letters.

All my sales letters were originally printed on my own standard letterhead, although I have recently moved to an 8.5" x 14" (legal size) format to make room for a fax-back reply coupon at the bottom. I use a laser printer for the most professional look. I suggest that you do, too.

Postcards and other self-mailers

Like sales letters, postcards are a form of direct mail, but they have some added advantages. They give you the opportunity to print full-color design at a relatively low cost and, in some jurisdictions, postcards are cheaper to mail than letters.

Brenda Kruse, the "Farm Girl" copywriter, uses postcards extensively to generate business and to promote her website, as does Seattle-based high-tech copywriting guru Janice King.

"I have had great success with postcards," reports Kruse. "Each year I develop a seasonal series of four that are mailed to around 800 prospects (agencies and companies). The cost is minimal, as is the printing. I get the benefits of multiple mailings at a fraction of the cost of doing a full-fledged brochure."

Cold calls

An online magazine recently featured articles written by two self-promotion gurus. These authors reportedly did not know each

Sample 4
LEAD-GENERATING SALES LETTER
(TARGETED AT AD AGENCIES AND DESIGN FIRMS)

This free INFORMATION KIT makes it easy to find the best copywriter for your B-to-B, DM projects

Dear Marketing Professional,

Chances are, you've lived through the following scenario:

A deadline for a important B-to-B, direct-mail project suddenly comes crashing around the corner ... and you're left scrambling to find a writer capable of delivering the strategy, copy, creative suggestions, and "wow" ideas you need for the job.

Now, I believe in saving clients time and hassle. So, I've put together a complete information kit that makes it easy for you to quickly assess my copywriting services. (After all, who needs the stress of frantic phone calls, meetings, and "book tours"?)

In this kit you'll find the following:

- Testimonials from clients like you (This takes the sting out of the question, "Can this guy deliver?")

- Samples of my work

- A Q&A (Answers to questions you may have such as, "What types of projects does he handle?" and "How easy Is he to work with?")

- A complete fee schedule (Great for budgeting.)

- Plus this bonus! A free copy of my recently published booklet: 59 *Tips for Creating Successful Internet Direct Mail.*

This information kit is yours for the asking. (So ask!) Simply give me a call toll free at 1-800-555-1234. I'll send it to you right away.

Best regards,

Steve Slaunwhite

Steve Slaunwhite

P.S. Why not ask for your information kit today? That way, when a deadline looms, you'll be glad to have all the information you need on my copywriting services at your fingertips.

The best book I ever read on cold calling was written by sales trainer Stephan Schiffman: *Cold-Calling Techniques (That Really Work!)*. It is short, practical, and straightforward. If you decide to try cold calling, I recommend this book.

Using sales letters and cold calls together is a powerful combination. After sending the letter, follow up with a phone call. This often doubles response.

other, nor did they realize they were submitting articles on the same topic to the same publication. I'm sure the editor decided to publish both in order to generate some buzz and readership. The first article was titled "How to Sell Your Services without Cold Calling." The second was called "How to Sell Your Services with Cold Calling."

Two experts. Two very different points of view. Hmm.

Cold calling has been the bane of every sales professional for eons. (I should know; as a sales rep early in my career, I made well over 2,000 cold calls, some of them very icy.) Cold calls are controversial. Some self-employed professionals swear by them, saying cold calls are the only way to reach clients and sell your services. Others insist it's a waste of time, and even undignified.

Sure, cold calling can be tough on the ego. But does it work? The answer is: Yes. But only if you have the skills and temperament to keep at it, and not take the rejection you're bound to face personally.

One well-known copywriter, Peter Bowerman, swears by this prospecting technique. In his book, *The Well-Fed Writer: Back For Seconds*, he writes "… cold calling should still be the cornerstone approach for this business — because it works." He goes on to advise that once you've given it an honest try, "It ceases to be an unpleasant garden-variety exercise in futility and morphs into a proven vehicle to success. You may never love it — not required — but even that may change when you see the impact on your bank account."

Other equally successful copywriters feel differently. "I'm a writer," says one professional, a big name in the direct marketing industry. "If I had to cold call to get business, I'd quit."

Strong feelings, on both sides.

Consider the advantages of cold calling:

- *It's inexpensive.* All you need is a phone. At today's long-distance telephone rates, you can reach potential clients across the country for pennies.

- *It's fast.* You don't wait for the post office to mail your sales letters, or the marketing magazine to publish your article. You can pick up the phone and reach dozens of prospects within a day.

- *It's revealing.* Even if you get a "No," you can learn a lot about the company, contacts, and future opportunities from a phone call — information you just can't get by sending a letter.

Now let's look at some disadvantages:

- *You hear all the "Nos."* Not everyone is polite. Some cold callers try to overcome this by reminding themselves that if they hear enough "Nos," they'll eventually hear a "Yes." That's true. But it may not make you feel any more confident.

- *It's time-consuming.* Mail some sales letters or place a few ads, and you're done. You can get onto other things. When making cold calls, however, you have to take the time to pick up the phone, dial it, and attempt to reach the right contacts. Typically, it takes an hour to make about 15 calls.

- *It's intimidating.* Even the most seasoned sales executive's stomach churns at the thought of doing some cold calls. Procrastination — usually manifested as staring at the phone endlessly as if it will dial itself — is typical. The best way to overcome this fear of cold calling is *just do it.* Make those first few calls. Often, the butterflies will go away.

Chris Marlow, known as "The Copywriter's Coach," is a big advocate of cold calling. Here's her advice on making calls effectively.

I teach my coaching students to create a Unique Selling Proposition (USP) for themselves, and then contact only those companies that strongly relate to that USP. The phone conversation might go something like this:

Copywriter: "I've been looking at your website for some time now and have been planning to call to check the spelling of your name and make sure you're at the Houston office so I can send you a letter ..."

Potential Client (who is flattered and curious): "Why have you been looking at our site?"

Copywriter: "Because you direct market Corvette parts and accessories and I am the world's only copywriter specializing solely in exotic cars. I felt that we were well matched."

Self-promotion — speaking at conferences, writing articles, networking — can harness the power of fame.

Potential Client: "Yes, it would seem so. We have to write most of our copy in house because we can't find anyone who can talk 'Corvette' or handle the technical aspect of the writing ..."

A "master salesman" knows that the highest conversion rates come from face-to-face selling. For the master copywriter, the corollary is one-to-one communication.

Marketing directors and agency creative directors understand the sales process and have heightened respect for the copywriter who follows its tenets ... as long as the message is relevant.

So if you've got the gift of aggressiveness, try cold calling. I promise that it will evolve from awkward and intimidating to fun and exciting in about ten calls. (In fact, the last time I cold called I got a "live one" on call number ten.)

If you think like a salesman and view it as a numbers game ("I must get nine "nos" so I can get to the one "yes"), you can become so engrossed in the process that getting a copy job feels like an interruption.

I like Chris's approach. However, it may be a bit aggressive for some people. In my experience, writers tend to be a shy bunch. I don't mean that as a put-down (I count myself as an introvert, too.) I just believe that not everyone is naturally gregarious enough to pick up the phone and call strangers over and over again.

Have I tried cold calling? I did years ago. Here is the script that I used:

"Hello, Mr. Smith? Hi, this is Steve Slaunwhite calling. I don't know whether or not you've heard of me, but I'm a copywriting expert for the software industry. I write sales letters, e-mail, and ads for companies like NCR, Hewlett-Packard, and Symantec, who need the highest response rates. Most professionals like yourself learn more about my services through an Information Kit that I send by e-mail. Would you like to receive one?"

That's it! I would dial the phone, ask for John Smith (or whoever), and say the above blurb as conversationally as possible. Then I would shut up. If John Smith said, "Yes," I would e-mail the information. If he said "No," I would politely say "Thank You," and hang up.

I suspect that telemarketing gurus would balk at my approach, probably saying that I give up too soon. But this script worked well for me. It was quick and fairly painless (by cold-calling standards, anyway), and I attracted some good clients.

Today, I don't have time to cold call. I'm too busy writing. But I still believe in this prospecting strategy. So I have someone else do it for me; a former professional sales person who works from home and freelances her services to self-employed professionals like me. I know other copywriters who also take this tact — outsourcing their calls to others. Hey, if you can't stomach cold calls yourself, there's absolutely nothing wrong with getting someone else to do it!

Advertising

Most of the copywriters that I have spoken with over the years have had only mixed results with ads. In fact, no one has ever shown me an advertisement for copywriting services — online or in print — that has been hugely successful. Yet, advertising can work well if you start small, notice what works, build on that success, and don't expect the Red Sea to part with just one placement.

For example, for a long time I noticed that a writer was placing an ongoing ad in a local marketing publication. It read, "Write for Hire," with a phone number. That was it. Not even the writer's name was included. Although I thought the copy could have been better, it must have been successful to some degree. After all, it ran week after week for more than two years. I suspect the reason for its longevity was that it generated enough work for the writer to pay for itself. Perhaps he or she received a predictable amount of enquiries per month, say three or four. This would have been reason enough to keep the ad in.

I don't advertise much. However, I do have a small ad that runs in *Inside Direct Mail* magazine. It costs me less than $300 per year and I get only a handful of enquiries from it. However, just one new job makes the investment more than worthwhile. This past year, for example, a company who had seen the ad called and they eventually hired me to write an e-mail campaign. My fee? $7,000.

That's the best way to approach advertising: modestly and carefully. Never waste your money on a big, splashy ad that costs you thousands. It might not generate any business for you. Start with

A sales representative for the world's most popular business directory — the *Yellow Pages* — once told me that the largest ad on the page generally gets called before any of the others.

modest ads, in targeted publications. Notice what works. Then build from there.

Where do you place your ads? It may seem like a good idea to pick general business publications. But in my experience, it isn't. A better choice is to promote your services in publications read by those who actually hire copywriters: marketing managers, creative directors, and so forth. (See Chapter 5 on target markets.)

Advertising in directories can also work well. My local marketing association publishes a directory every year featuring advertising agencies, lettershops, creative firms, freelancers, consultants, and others who provide products and services to the marketing community.

I have found that almost every industry has a directory that is the "bible" of that industry; the guide everyone turns to when seeking help. So, if you're targeting a specific industry with your copywriting services, make enquiries. Ask prospective clients and others which directory they turn to most.

Most directories will list your copywriting services at no charge, usually with a limit on word count, size, and format. If you want more space, color, and design, you pay. This can make directory advertising very cheap or very expensive, depending on which way you go. If a modest listing in a particular directory does well for you, you might consider a bigger, glossy placement.

Experiment with different prospecting methods. You may wish to use a worksheet such as the one in Sample 5 to track your efforts.

Articles

Getting articles published in magazines, newsletters, journals, and e-zines is a very effective means of prospecting for clients. When people read your article, they see you as an expert. And you are, because you've taken the time to research, learn, organize, and write on your topic.

Writing articles can create awareness and generate enquiries for your copywriting business. Editors are always looking for article ideas and contributions from experts, mainly because readers like hearing what experts have to say. Usually, these editors are more than willing to include a short promotional blurb on your services

Sample 5
PROSPECTING TRACKING FORM

Advertising

Publication: *Marketing Promotions*

Type of ad: *⅛ page — 2-color*

Date of issue: *Sept 20--*

Cost per placement: *$225*

Name of ad: *"Power Packed Proposals"*

Results: *Inquiries* ~~HHH~~

Orders |

Sales Letters

Type: *8½ x 14 Faxback sales letter*

Cost per piece: *$0.22 plus postage*

Amount mailed: *200*

List: *Compiled from business directory*

Target market: *Maketing managers*

Name of mailing: *"Free information kit"*

Results: *Calls/inquiries* ~~HHH~~ |

Fax (leads) ||

Phone calls

Calls per day/session: *10*

Total per week/period: *50*

Script name: *"Portfolio update"*

List: *In-house list*

Target market: *Old leads, old clients*

Results: *Reached:* ~~HHH~~ ~~HHH~~ ||

New leads: ||||

"Speaking in public creates a positive visibility, boosts your credibility, and establishes you as an expert in your field," says C.J. Hayden, author of *Get Clients Now!* "It puts you in direct contact with potential clients in a powerful way."

at the end of the article. Here's an example of a bio that doubles as advertisement:

> *Steve Slaunwhite is one of the top copywriting experts in software marketing. He writes sales letters, DM packages, e-mails, landing pages, web pages, brochures, sell sheets, case studies, newsletters, and other communications that get leads and make sales — often in record numbers. Steve can be reached at <www.steveslaunwhite.com>.*

I suggest you develop a list of ten or so publications that you can approach with your article ideas. Magazines aimed at sales and marketing professionals tend to work best, as opposed to general business publications.

Don't just look on the bookstore magazine shelf. Most membership associations publish newsletters, as do many corporations. There are also hundreds of e-zines (online newsletters) and content websites available that are always looking for articles. One piece I wrote, "9 More Tips for Successful E-mail Marketing," was published by more than 20 online publications.

Contact editors and publishers. Ask how to best approach them with article ideas. Check out their websites. There may be links to an editorial calendar (a schedule of planned topics for upcoming issues) and writer's guidelines for submissions.

When pitching an article idea to an editor, a one- to two-page "query letter" is the standard approach — especially if you've never written for that publication before. Consult Sample 6 for ways to extend the promotional life of the articles you write.

Speaking

Like articles, a presentation to a group that includes potential clients — creative directors, marketing managers, or business owners — positions you as an expert and a player. There are few self-promotion activities you can do that will build your credibility faster. Bob Bly, perhaps the world's most successful all-round copywriter, once told me, "Do it right, and a speech will always get you a new client."

Sample 6
GETTING MORE MILEAGE FROM YOUR ARTICLES

Once you have an article published, don't let it languish in an issue of a single publication. You can extend its promotional life in a variety of ways. Here are some suggestions for getting more mileage from the articles you write:

1. Post a copy on your website.

2. Submit it to other website owners for publication in their e-zine.

3. Mail or e-mail a copy to colleagues, prospects, and clients.

4. Use it as a handout when you speak before a group.

5. Recycle the content into other articles and book sections.

6. Combine articles into a special report and offer it as a giveaway in your sales letters and other prospecting efforts.

7. Include a copy with your brochure.

8. Republish it as a small brochure or tip sheet.

9. Send a copy to others who write similar articles. (They may quote you!)

10. Send a copy of your article with your invoice.*

* This tip comes from C.J. Hayden's book *Get Clients Now!* It seems so simple and natural that I'm stunned I never thought of it. Great idea — and one I will use.

Bonus Tip:

Since the last edition of *Start & Run a Copywriting Business*, some readers have complained that it's difficult to get their articles published in top-tier marketing magazines such as *Target Marketing* and *Inside Direct Mail*. Here's a tip: If you can't get in the front door with your article, try the back door instead with a "Letter to the Editor." These are often easier to get published.

To improve your speaking skills, take Peter Urs Bender's advice from his book *Secrets of Power Presentations*: "The best and simplest way to improve is to pay attention to other presenters and analyze what they do. Observe the great ones and also the beginners. Determine what it is that makes the good ones good and the bad ones bad."

Associations and professional organizations that hold monthly and annual meetings are continually looking for speakers and presenters. If you are interested in speaking at a meeting, develop a 30- to 45-minute talk on a topic related to your expertise — copywriting and marketing, for example. Then contact the event planner or education director of some of the local groups and ask if you can present at an upcoming event. You're sure to get a positive response.

Afraid to speak in public? Join the club. We've got jackets! Survey after survey suggests that most people fear public speaking even more than death. The best cure is preparation and practice. Prepare a solid presentation and know it inside and out, and anticipate any questions you might receive from the audience. Then take the leap. The more you speak, the more confident you'll feel. As one professional speaker once told me, "The butterflies may not go away, but they do start to fly in formation."

Networking

If you have an outgoing personality, networking may be your ticket. There are hundreds of conferences, meetings, trade shows, and other events that are frequented by potential clients for your copywriting services.

If you like to socialize, enjoy meeting new people, and are not afraid to introduce yourself to strangers, then networking can be a great way to prospect. If you're on the shy side, however, you can still be effective in networking situations — but you may not enjoy it much.

When I go to a meeting or event attended by potential clients, I make it a goal to introduce myself to three people. They may be prospects, or they may not be. It doesn't matter. The fact that I have taken the initiative is the important point. Once I have met three new people, I relax.

I never try to overtly sell my service to the folks I meet in networking situations. I find this pushy and intrusive. Instead, I simply introduce myself, tell them what I do, then ask what *they* do. That's key. Be more interested in the person your speaking with than in promoting your services. If they, in turn, are interested in what you do, they'll ask.

When telling people in networking situations what it is that you do, answer clearly and in as few words as possible. No one wants to listen to an elaborate pitch of your services. At least, not yet. Renowned sales trainer Tom Stoyan suggests starting with the statement, "I specialize in … " then going on to describe what you do, along with one or two key benefits, using no more than 20 words.

Here's an example:

Hi, I'm Debra. I specialize in helping marketing professionals leverage the selling power of words. In short, I'm a freelance copywriter.

Most people will remember what you do if you can keep your introduction short, but impactful. If you're remembered, you'll have a greater chance of receiving referrals and leads from your networking efforts. See Sample 7 for ways to cultivate referrals.

What's your prospecting personality?

"I hate prospecting," a struggling copywriter complained to me recently. "I know I have to make cold calls to get clients, but every time I sit down at the phone I break out into a cold sweat."

"Then stop cold calling," I said.

My answer surprised him. Perhaps it surprises you, too? After all, aren't you supposed to do some uncomfortable things to get your name in front of potential clients?

Not necessarily.

It makes no sense to do something you hate, even if it works. Because if you hate it, you won't do it consistently. (Consistency is the whole secret behind successful prospecting.)

Prospecting isn't something you do just when business is slow. It must be woven indelibly into your business life, like bookkeeping and reading the trade magazines. You need to fish for new clients monthly, weekly, or even daily. If you don't, you'll become infinitely acquainted with the phrase: "Feast or famine."

So how do you prospect regularly without losing your mind? My advice is to find a method that matches your personality. For example, do you like mingling? Schmoozing? Chatting people up?

Sales trainer Tom Stoyan, who built his training business almost entirely from networking, warns, "Don't try to sell your services when you first meet people. Instead, focus on how you can help them or their company." Tom also advises, "Don't run around a meeting collecting business cards. Although the by-product of effective networking results in new contacts, networking is not a numbers game."

Sample 7
CULTIVATING REFERRALS

I never directly ask for referrals, and I suggest you don't, as it places clients in an awkward position. But I do make it as easy as possible for clients to refer me. Here are some ideas:

1. *Refer others.* You are more likely to get referrals if you give them.

2. *Be likeable.* It sounds trite, but people tend to refer people they like. No one wants to pawn off an unpleasant, difficult, or grumpy freelancer to a friend.

3. *Meet deadlines.* No client will refer you to others if you miss deadlines, no matter how wonderful your work is.

4. *Solve problems quickly.* Clients will not refer you if they have a poor experience with your services, or see you as the source of a problem. Bad memories last. If your clients present you with a problem in the copy you submitted, fix it promptly — and with a smile.

5. *Say thanks.* I always send a personal thank-you e-mail when I receive a referral. I also remember to say thank you again when speaking to the client by phone.

6. *Ask for feedback.* I continually ask clients for their opinion on my copywriting. Interestingly, the very act of asking for feedback often prompts clients to give me a referral.

Clients aren't the only source of referrals. Freelance designers, marketing consultants, editors, and even other copywriters can also recommend your services to others.

Then, as we've learned earlier in this chapter, networking can be very effective. A corporate writer I know built his business from the ground up primarily by hanging out at business meetings and conferences. "I get nervous initially when I attend a networking event," he told me recently. "That's normal. But once I've introduced myself to a couple of people, it becomes fun."

Writing is another great prospecting strategy, and one most copywriters are comfortable with. After all, writing is what we do best.

There are many ways you can use words to reach potential clients. Getting articles published in magazines, newsletters, journals, and e-zines are the most popular methods. You can also write sales letters, press releases, special reports, and even ads.

You might want to also determine if speaking falls within your comfort zone. By the way, if you think you can't lead a presentation before a group because you're an introvert, think again. It's amazing how many so-called shy people are professional speakers!

Cold calling is the prospecting method that even the most thick-skinned among us loathe. A recent report by MarketingSherpa (an online marketing information service) revealed that in business-to-business prospecting, cold calls are the fastest way to reach and convert new clients. It may be the fastest, but it can be a rough ride. Most folks will try to brush you off. A few may even hang up, rudely. It comes with the territory.

So you can write, talk, network, or call your way to more clients. All these methods work extremely well. Pick one or two that you'll enjoy doing most. Then do the work. And keep doing it. Never stop.

Creating the Perfect Fulfillment Plan

When a potential client responds to your sales letter or call and asks, "How do I learn more about your services?", what do you do? Obviously, you're going to need a way to fulfill that request. Hence, a fulfillment plan.

When I got started, I offered clients a thick Information Kit that included a client list, testimonials, reprints of articles I've published, a list of books I've written, a "Q&A" on my services, and more. It was expensive to print, put together, and send out, but it worked.

These days, because of the Internet, I do things differently. In fact, I no longer have printed marketing materials (except business cards and letterhead).

Most of the material that was in my original printed Information Kit is now on my website, so potential clients can get much of what they need there.

I have also developed an e-mail version of my original Information Kit, so I can send prospects additional materials that I don't want to post on my website. For example, a fee schedule, response analysis of marketing pieces I've written, and detailed samples of my work.

Putting together strong fulfillment materials — whether print-based or electronically published — at the start of your business is a difficult challenge. One of the problems is that most beginning copywriters do not have their business clearly defined when they start out. I know I didn't. One copywriter told me about the costly mistake she made by printing her hourly fee in her brochure. A few weeks later, she realized she wasn't charging enough and was forced to raise her fees. When she did, all those expensive brochures went straight into the trash. Ouch!

But the Internet does make things a lot easier these days. You can create your fulfillment materials online as a website. Then, when you need to make changes — and you will, as your business evolves — you simply upload revised text.

If you decide to produce a brochure or other printed materials, keep it simple, especially during your first months in business. Things will change — your prices, services, even contact information. You'll want to be able to incorporate these changes quickly and inexpensively. So a glossy, multipage exposé on your services, at least at the beginning, is probably not a good idea.

Here's a tip: Instead of a brochure, put together a folder of information on your services, made up of loose inserts. That way, if you need to update something, you only need to revise and print a new insert rather than your entire fulfillment package.

What do prospective clients want to know about your copywriting services? Here's a handy checklist of what to address in your fulfillment materials:

- ❑ What do you do?
- ❑ What are your qualifications?
- ❑ Do you have experience in our industry?
- ❑ Do you have experience with our kind of product or service?
- ❑ Do you have experience writing copy that sells to our target audience?
- ❑ Who are your clients?
- ❑ What do your clients say about your services?
- ❑ What assurance do we have that you can deliver great copy?
- ❑ How do we hire you?
- ❑ Will you deliver finished copy by the deadline?
- ❑ How do you handle revisions?
- ❑ What about design and production?
- ❑ How much do you charge?
- ❑ How can we see samples of your work?
- ❑ Why should I hire you over another copywriter?
- ❑ What is the process of working with you?

My fulfillment package — my website, augmented by customized information sent by e-mail — currently includes:

- What I do
- Types of projects I handle
- Types of clients I work with
- Client list
- Client testimonials
- Fee schedule
- Reprints of articles I've published

One of my goals for my information package is to help a prospect feel comfortable enough to immediately hire my services without feeling the need to schedule a live meeting.

I send prospective clients a package of information, rather than a brochure. A package seems more valuable than a brochure. And it is.

- My bio

- FAQ on my services

- Response figures I've written for marketing campaigns

- Samples of my work

Now, you may not have all this information in *your* fulfillment package, especially if you're just starting out. Don't worry. Put together the best information you can, in the most presentable format possible. Build slowly. Tune in to what clients need to know most about you and your services. Notice what works, and what doesn't. Showcase your strengths. Don't be afraid to ask potential clients what they like about your fulfillment materials, and what they didn't like. Their answers are often revealing.

How to get clients to say nice things about you — in writing

Testimonials are a powerful addition to any fulfillment plan. In fact, so many other freelance copywriters include endorsements in their marketing materials that yours may seem conspicuous without them.

How do you go about gathering client testimonials? Start by realizing that you do have clients who want to say nice things about your services — they just may not have the time to sit down and write you a letter or e-mail. So, you can help them by making this easier.

Here's an approach that almost always works for me. When I successfully complete a project for a client who is obviously happy with my services, I send an e-mail requesting feedback. Sample 8 is an example of such a request.

I try to time the sending of this e-mail to coincide with the print or electronic publication of the project I just completed. I figure I stand a better chance of receiving a favorable reply if the client received my request while gushing over her new website or brochure.

Here's another strategy that also works very well. Often, clients will review your copy and then send you an e-mail with comments. These can include, "Nice job," "I like the way you organized this.

Sample 8
REQUEST FOR FEEDBACK

Subject Line: Your opinion?

John,

Thanks for asking me to contribute to the EdgeWare Dynamo direct-mail project. I enjoyed working with you and your staff very much.

Now, I have a favor to ask.

Currently, I'm in the process of collecting client testimonials ... and I'd like to hear from you!

Could you take a moment and give me your opinion of my services? No need to write a formal letter — simply reply to this e-mail with any comments you think appropriate.

Of course, I'd be delighted to read your positive comments — but I also welcome any suggestions or criticisms, too.

Thanks,

Steve Slaunwhite
Steve Slaunwhite

I map out my contact strategy on my computer using contact management software. Currently, I use *ACT!*, but there are others that are just as good. The software stores the necessary contact information and prompts me to make the next step in the follow-up process. It remembers for me, so I never have to wonder, "Should I give this prospect a call, or should I wait another month?"

Of course, you don't need software to sketch out your follow-up strategy. You can use an appointment book, organizer, wall chart, calendar — anything that works.

Very effective!" or "This sales letter looks great. We can't wait to test it." When you receive unsolicited accolades like these, reply back with something like: "Thanks for the feedback, Joan. By the way, may I share your comments with others as a client testimonial?" If Joan says "Yes," you've got it.

Creating an Effective Keep-in-Touch Plan

Here's what can often happen. A prospective client meets you at a networking event, or comes across your website on the Internet, or replies to your call or letter. She's impressed with your samples and experience. She says she's going to hire you, the very next chance she gets. "In about three months," she says, "I'll have a project for you." So you wait. Three months go by. Nothing happens. You call and, oh my gosh, she's hired someone else.

What happened? Well, she could have just been acting polite, not really intending to use your services. But more likely she simply forgot about you. These days, clients are extremely busy. They're juggling numerous projects; working late; dealing with dozens of vendors, consultants, and other freelancers; and traveling. A letter, e-mail, or package they received from you three months earlier may have slipped out of sight, out of mind.

So how do you stay on the radar screen? The answer is to have an effective keep-in-touch plan.

There's a fine line between keeping in touch and being a pest. As one well-known copywriter put it during a teleseminar I attended recently, "Clients will respect a freelancer that perseveres, but not one that annoys."

How do you determine when to follow up with a client, how often, and by which means? That's easy. You simply ask. Say to a prospective client, "Joan, how do you prefer that I keep in touch? By phone? E-mail? A little of both?" You can ask questions about the frequency. For example, "Joan, does following-up about every six weeks or so make sense to you? Or should I keep in touch more frequently?"

Many copywriters are surprised when I suggest that they ask a prospective client how they would prefer the follow-up process to work. Some have asked, "Steve, if I ask the prospect these questions, won't some say not to follow up at all?" Yes, some may.

But in my experience, these won't make good prospects for you anyway. So they're actually doing you a favor. Those that do say, "Sure, keep in touch every six weeks by e-mail" tend to be much better prospects for future work.

I read many years ago that it takes an average of seven contacts with a prospect over time before your name becomes front-of-mind. That's exactly where you want to be — the first person a prospective client thinks about when she needs a copywriter.

When keeping in touch, take a helpful approach. If you come across an article on generating sales leads — a topic your prospect is interested in — call or send an e-mail letting her know. You can clip and mail the article; a very effective strategy hardly anyone uses. Recently, I came across an article on how to attract affluent vacationers to high-end resorts. One of my prospects was just such a hotelier, so I photocopied the piece and faxed it to him. On the cover page of the fax, I simply wrote, "John, here's an article that might interest you. Steve." Two weeks later, he called and offered me an assignment.

Ten ways to stay in touch with prospects

The following list includes ten ways that you can stay in touch with prospects:

1. Send a letter.

2. Send a postcard.

3. Send an e-mail.

4. Send a fax.

5. Make a special offer (e.g., a free booklet).

6. Send a press release.

7. Leave a voice mail. (You'll reach a prospect's voice mail 70 percent of the time. Make good use of it!)

8. Send them helpful information (e.g., articles, reports, tips, checklists).

9. Refer them to others. (Prospects rarely forget someone who has sent a potential client their way.)

10. Say "Hello" at a meeting, seminar, or event.

Approach every assignment as if it is your first with the client.

Remember, Each Assignment Earns the Next

What is the most powerful way to build your income? Generate repeat business? Get more referrals? Command higher fees? It's simple: Do a great job. Being able to consistently deliver good copy to your clients — on time — is the number-one reason clients will give you more work, and refer you to others.

Never get complacent with a client simply because you've been working with him or her for a few months — or a few years — and feel you're well established. You're not. Always be professional, and deliver the best work you can on every project. Never stop impressing your client.

7
The Fine Art of Quoting

Knowing how much to charge for a particular copywriting assignment is often an arduous business task for freelance copywriters. One reason is that fees for freelancers vary tremendously. Some copywriting fees I have come across are ridiculously cheap; others astonishingly expensive. Some copywriters bill by the hour; others charge a fixed fee per project.

Fees vary by assignment: Direct mail and annual reports pay better than brochures and newsletters. Fees vary by geography: copywriters in California may charge more on average than copywriters in Vermont. So pricing your services fairly and competitively isn't easy. In fact, it's not uncommon to agonize over a particular quote for an hour before you hold your breath and send it in.

According to copywriter and writing coach Steve Manning, "If you've got a problem quoting on jobs, welcome to the club ... we've now got jackets. Don't worry about it ... you'll always be wrong. Ask for more than you think is appropriate. Ask for more than you think the client will pay. Then wonder how much money you left on the table when the client says, 'go ahead.'"

Develop a Fee Schedule

One of the best tools for helping you quote sufficiently to meet your needs and those of your clients is to develop a fee schedule. A fee schedule is simply a list of estimated fees for typical copywriting assignments. When a client calls, instead of guessing and stumbling through impromptu calculations, you can consult your fee schedule. This makes quoting a much easier and more accurate process.

I constantly update my fee schedule based on what I learn about the value of particular assignments and how much work is involved in completing them. Sales letters, for example, do not take me a great deal of time to write. But their value to most clients is high, so I price them accordingly. For a long while, websites did not pay well. Businesses were focusing more on flashy graphics and funky functionality than on copy. But this is changing and clients are now paying closer attention to content, so website copywriters are finally being paid their due.

Determining fees for typical copywriting assignments isn't easy. One way to do this is to be sneaky: Pose as a potential client and call a few unsuspecting freelancers for rates. This approach is common in many industries. In fact, there's even a special name for it that sounds better than lying: Competitive shopping.

A more honest approach is to ask freelancers you know for assistance in putting together your fee schedule. Some freelance copywriters publish their rates on their website, which is handy. You might convince a freelancer friend to give you a fee range for a few typical projects.

You can also call a designer or ad agency pro you know and ask what they pay freelancers for typical assignments. Ask, "What do expensive copywriters charge?" This approach will often yield a few examples and a couple of "high fee" horror stories, and will help you determine the ceiling for your rates.

If you can get the scoop on fees for just one or two typical projects, it won't take you long to piece together a rough fee schedule. Once you have this, you can hone it as you learn more about the rates for your market.

Writer's Market, an annual freelance writers' marketing guide, publishes a schedule of typical fees based on feedback from their subscribers. This is a thick, annual publication, so the information is fairly up-to-date. It provides examples of both US and Canadian rates.

I have found keeping an up-to-date fee schedule invaluable when quoting on projects — especially when I am unable to determine a client's budget or how much he or she is willing to pay. If I receive an inquiry to write a brochure, for example, I simply look at my fee schedule, see that I charge between $350 and $600 a panel, and quote accordingly.

I also include my fee schedule in the information kit I send to potential clients. This way, when clients call me, they already know the range of my fees, which goes a long way in eliminating "sticker shock," and filtering out those clients unable to pay professional-level fees (my fees are at the high end of the scale).

Another way to estimate fees and create a fee schedule for your services is to guess. I did a lot of guessing at the beginning of my freelance career, and you will too.

Don't base your fees on less than $50 an hour, even if you're just starting out. You might think you can get more assignments because you're inexpensive, but you won't. Most clients equate low rate with cut rate. They'll think, perhaps accurately, that you are a beginner and an amateur — or not good enough to command higher fees. Recently, a client admitted that he awarded me a project because I was expensive. "If you're able to get these fees," he concluded, "you must be good."

The fee schedule in Sample 9 is based on an informal survey of freelance copywriters and clients in the greater Toronto area. Fees for top copywriters will be higher than those listed here. Beginners may charge below the lower end of the range. In my estimation, these fees represent an average of what copywriters generally charge in my market.

Hourly Rate or Fixed Fee?

Whether to quote an hourly or a fixed fee per project is a controversial topic in freelancing. A friend of mine, another freelancer, insists on quoting by the hour. She feels her chances of being "ripped off" are just too great to quote a fixed, all-inclusive project fee. By billing hourly, she points out, she is assured of being paid for every minute she puts into the project, and that a client will not take advantage of her time. She further insists that quoting an hourly rate is fairer to her clients. If a project takes less time for her to complete than expected, her client is charged less.

Sample 9
FEE SCHEDULE

Below are estimated average fees charged by full-time freelance copywriters. Some professionals charge more, others less, depending on their experience and track record. Fees quoted are in US dollars.

Print advertisement (full page)	$500–$2,000
Print advertisement (partial page)	$500–$1,000
Advertorial	$500–$1,000/page
Sales letter (1–2 pages)	$750–$1,500
Sales letter (multiple pages)	$750–$1,000/page
Direct-mail package (to generate leads)	$1,500–$3,500+
Direct-mail package (to generate sales)	$2,500–$5,000+
Self-mailer (postcard or folded)	$750–$2,000
Teleselling phone script	$750–$2,000
Website (home page)	$750–$1,500
Website (other pages)	$500–$750
E-zine ad	$500–$750
Banner ad	$500–$750
Landing page	$750–$1,500
Microsite	$750–$1,000/page
E-mail marketing (short form)	$500–$1,000
E-mail marketing (long form)	$1,000–$2,500
Brochures	$500–$750/page
Catalogs	$200–$350/item
Press releases	$500–$750
Newsletter or e-zine articles	$750–$1,000
Case studies.	$750–$1,500
Sales proposals	$1,500–$2,500+
PowerPoint scripts	$75–$150/slide

I disagree. For me, quoting an hourly rate creates far more problems than it solves. Sure, there are some advantages to quoting hourly. But I believe the disadvantages far exceed the advantages. Decide for yourself. Below is a comparison of hourly rates versus fixed fees.

Hourly rate: You must estimate the total hours you will spend working on the project.

Fixed fee: You quote a fixed fee for the project, regardless of hours spent.

When you quote an hourly rate, you will have to estimate a total cost for your services. No client is going to write you a blank check. So regardless of the time you spend on the project, your final invoice will still need to be relatively close to your original estimate. If it isn't, you'll have to provide your client with a good argument as to why you went over budget. Your client may argue back. And now you're involved in a billing dispute, which doesn't do much to further client relations.

When you quote a fixed fee, there is little possibility of a billing dispute. That's because your client knows upfront how much he or she is paying for your services. If you have quoted $750 for a small brochure, that's what your final invoice will read.

Hourly rate: Clients cannot take advantage of your time.

Fixed fee: You may find yourself at a client's beck and call for the duration of the project.

When you charge an hourly rate, your client is billed for your time spent answering his or her phone calls, attending his or her meetings, and completing his or her revisions. So you don't have to worry that you will not be paid for the hours you put into the project. If your client is overly demanding, requests endless revisions, wastes your time, or is an unrelenting nag, at least you can take comfort in knowing that you're being paid for every hour of it.

But there's a downside to this advantage. When you bill hourly, your clients may feel that every time they call you to discuss a project, they're on the toll. As a copywriter who charges by the hour, you may constantly field requests like, "I need a small revision. Is this going to cost me more?" The last thing you want is your client

When quoting a fixed fee, state that revisions are free, not that they are included. If you say your revisions are included in your fixed fee, and there are no revision requests, your clients may ask for a discount.

When quoting a fixed fee, be sure to factor in anticipated meetings, discussions, revisions, and expenses.

to feel timid about calling on your expertise and services. After a while, he or she might decide you're not worth the trouble.

Another disadvantage is that you may find yourself constantly discussing your fees for the duration of the project. I once got a call from an ad agency executive who told me he was sick of calling his freelance copywriter to discuss revisions and other project details only to be greeted with, "You realize this is going to cost you more?"

When you quote a fixed fee, the fee negotiations are completed upfront. That's it! No more discussion! (Unless, of course, the nature of the project fundamentally changes.) For the rest of the project, your client focuses on the great work you do — not the fees you charge.

Hourly rate: You charge only for the hours you have actually worked.

Fixed fee: If you work productively and efficiently, you are rewarded.

Here's another problem I have with hourly fees: If you work productivity and efficiently, shouldn't you be rewarded? Conversely, if you decide to be lazy and inefficient — racking up hours with little to show for it — why should your client have to pay? When I lived in a condominium, a plumbing contractor showed up one day to rechalk my bathtub. Since he was being paid hourly by the condominium board, he decided to milk the job. It took him three hours to complete work it would take an amateur half the time to do. He worked so slowly that it was actually painful to watch!

I work hard to be productive and efficient. If I improve my skills and process to be able to complete a great brochure in less time, why should I earn less? After all, clients are interested in the value I bring to a project and what I can deliver, not how much time I spend on the project. So I quote for value, not time.

Hourly rate: You will experience more price objections.

Fixed fee: You will experience fewer price objections.

It's a curious fact that clients are more agreeable to paying $900 for a sales letter, than $90 per hour for ten hours' work. This is partly because many clients don't understand how the $90 per hour rate was arrived at to begin with. They may not appreciate your costs of doing business — marketing, accounting, office expense. Worse, they may naturally compare your rates to their own income, or that of their employees. They may think, "I'm paying this guy $90 per hour! Ouch!"

Clients can more easily relate to a fixed fee than an hourly fee. Think about it. If one kid on your block offers to mow your lawn for a $10 flat rate, and another offers to do it for $7 per hour, which would you hire? Even if you're certain the lawn requires only an hour or so of work, most people would feel more comfortable with the flat rate. At least you know exactly what you're paying.

Your client may also have difficulty relating your hourly rate to the value of the project. Compelling website copy may very well be worth $1,200 to your client, but when you break that amount into hourly segments, the value link is broken. In fact, you're not selling value anymore, you're submitting a punch card.

Hourly rates can also create problems when a client asks for a break in the price. If you bill by the hour, you'll have to reduce your hourly rate. Once your client knows he or she can get your services at $70 per hour, he or she will ask for that rate again — I guarantee it. Of course, a similar problem can happen when you quote a fixed fee, but it's easier to deal with.

Hourly rate: Your income is limited to your hourly rate times the hours you worked.

Fixed fee: Your income is limited only to your personal productivity and the value you provide to clients.

From an income perspective, quoting an hourly rate severely limits you. If your rate is $50 per hour, and you work 30 hours each week on client projects (remember, you'll need to spend time on other non-billable tasks such as bookkeeping and marketing), your income is limited to $67,500. Not bad. But you could have earned more by quoting a fixed price per project.

It's interesting to note that very few of the top freelance copywriters I interviewed for this book quote an hourly rate. Almost all quote a fixed fee per project.

Hourly rate: Most clients do not like to pay an hourly rate.

Fixed fee: Most clients prefer a fixed fee.

To your client, there is a real advantage in receiving a fixed fee for your services. For example, if you quote $1,200 for a website, rather than $90 per hour for 13 hours, they can confidently plug your quote into their budget. This immediately puts you on their "easy to work with" list, which could mean more assignments in the future. Your fixed fee also helps them to get budgets approved faster, which gets you the assignment sooner.

When you quote an hourly rate, however, you become an unpredictable element in the project. The client worries about budget overruns, even if you promise to stay within your estimate. You make it more difficult for the client to do business with you, which could affect how much business you receive.

Is hourly versus fixed fees really such a big issue for clients? When I ask my clients what they like about my services, the number one thing, next to the quality of copy I write for them, is my all-inclusive fee structure.

Hourly rate: More practical on larger projects.

Fixed fee: Less practical on larger projects.

There are, of course, some situations where quoting a fixed fee is unpractical — even impossible. I was once awarded an assignment to write a very large e-commerce website for a client who had no idea how many screens or how much information would need to be included. Because there was no way of determining upfront the true scope of the project, I quoted an hourly rate with a total cost estimate.

Most copywriting projects — ads, direct mail, brochures, web pages — are relatively short. But if you're faced with an arduous and long assignment (such as a multipage booklet or a corporate website) then quoting an hourly rate may be unavoidable.

Factors to Consider when Quoting Assignments

Don't make the mistake of quoting a project based solely on number of pages, word count, or other project size and scope details. There are plenty of other factors to consider before committing to a price. Remember, once you have quoted a job and accepted the assignment, it's very difficult — perhaps impossible — to request more money from the client.

You need to dig deep to avoid under-quoting a job — and subsequently working harder and longer on a project than you anticipated. There is nothing more miserable than hacking away at a project and realizing you made an error quoting and won't be getting paid what you should for the job.

Consider the following factors before you quote on a client project.

Meetings

How many off-site meetings will you have to attend to successfully complete the job? Can project information be exchanged by e-mail, phone, teleconferencing, and courier? Will you have to attend an initial briefing? What about progress meetings? Will you have to travel to a meeting every time the client wants to discuss an outline, a draft, or revisions?

Despite the communications revolution, corporate clients still love to schedule meetings. But for you, traveling to attend a meeting at a client's office is time-consuming and expensive. If you suspect a project is going to require your attendance at meetings, quote accordingly.

Better still, try to convince your client to use other communication channels. When a client calls me to ask for a meeting, I often say, "Let's save time and discuss your project now. If you need me to see a document, you can send it by e-mail or courier." Sometimes, I will pay the courier expense or the teleconferencing fee to avoid a meeting. The few dollars I spend is a cheap price compared to the two- to three-hour time loss of traveling across town to a meeting.

The deadline

Once you have a few freelance copywriting jobs under your belt, you'll have a good idea of how long it takes to complete certain assignments. This will help you negotiate deadlines with clients and schedule sufficient time to work at a comfortable, relatively stress-free pace.

However, you're bound to receive many calls from clients who want you to meet tough — sometimes unbelievable — deadlines. This is especially true of ad agencies and design firms, which tend to work at a frenetic pace. You'll receive requests such as, "I need this brochure written by the end of this week. Can you handle it?"

A rush rate is a higher fee applied to extremely tight deadlines. This can vary, but the average is a 50 percent to 100 percent premium on your normal fees.

Some clients will even expect you to work evenings and weekends. It's not uncommon to receive a request on Friday for a job due the following Monday.

If you're among the few who get energized by rush jobs and tough deadlines, great. But many of us are not. So when you are asked to tackle a project with an impossible timeline, you have every right to charge more.

Keep in mind, however, that if a client gives you a reasonable deadline, but you must work evenings and weekends because of the volume of work you have taken on, this isn't the client's fault. It's yours. So your rush rate doesn't apply here.

You don't *have* to accept rush jobs. I have a policy of not accepting any assignment with a deadline of less than a full week — no matter how small the job is. I will break this rule, however, for very good clients if I can complete the job successfully and deliver quality work in the time available. But this is becoming rarer these days.

Type of industry

If you have proven experience in certain industries, you can charge a premium for your copywriting services. For example, copywriters who have good technical and marketing knowledge of high technology, investment services, insurance, or pharmaceuticals can command top fees for associated projects. If this is you, and you can prove your expertise, quote accordingly.

The technical complexity of the project

Some projects will require you to get your head around some tough technical acronyms, buzzwords, and concepts. You'll have to read through a pile of documents, track down contacts and ask questions, study the technical features and benefits until you understand them at least as well as your client does. This all takes time.

Even if you're already technically savvy, marketing projects for technical products take extra work to complete. Usually, they are "long copy" assignments because more text is needed to explain the features and benefits. Brochures, websites, and even print ads for complex products and services tend to have more copy and fewer visuals. So you should charge accordingly.

But such projects are also an opportunity to learn and expand your knowledge — information you can leverage on other projects with other clients. Your enhanced knowledge of data networking, for example, could serve you well in getting more clients within the vast networking and data communications industry. Financial services, especially insurance and investments, also qualify as technically complex products and are huge markets for copywriters. So you might consider some of the extra work you do on these types of projects as tuition.

Is your client an agency or a design firm?

If you are being offered an assignment from an ad agency or design firm, they will likely be marking up your fee when they invoice their client. So you'll be somewhat restricted as to how much you can quote. Generally, I have found that copywriting fees for agency clients are 20 percent to 30 percent less than for direct clients.

This doesn't mean you get a 20 percent windfall when you work for direct clients. Direct clients — whether they are corporations, associations, government, or nonprofits — often require more attention. Remember, when you work for an agency, they will handle most of the client contact. When you work direct, you're on your own.

Size of client

Larger clients tend to have larger budgets. They can afford to pay professional rates for professional work. Small-business clients, however, are more price sensitive. You can certainly quote your normal corporate rate to a small-business client, but be prepared not to get the job.

Personally, I don't quote a lower rate to smaller businesses. Why should they get a break when my larger clients pay full fee? I simply quote my standard rate and let the chips fall where they may.

Type of project

You can charge more for some copywriting assignments than for others. Mail order, lead-generating direct mail, Internet direct mail, corporate annual reports, and sales letters are among the top-paying assignments in copywriting. If you have had a demonstrated success with these types of project, you can — and should — charge more. (You deserve it.)

While television commercials no doubt pay very well, they are almost always handled by ad agencies, specialty firms, and producer-writer teams. Few copywriters I know get involved in this type of work.

In Chapter 11 of this book you'll find some advice on how to respond when a client objects to your quoted fee. See the section entitled "Help! My client complains my quote is too high!"

Copywriting tasks that pay moderately more than others include brochures, websites, case studies, media packages, newsletters, press releases, packaging copy, and video scripts.

Negotiating Your Fee

The best way to begin the process of quoting is simply to ask your clients, "How much did you budget for this particular job?" In some cases, they will tell you exactly how much they are expecting to pay, and you will know how much to quote (assuming, of course, their budget falls comfortably within your fee range).

But if your client does not have a set budget for the copywriting work — or does, but doesn't want to tell you — you're going to have to do some mind reading. Fortunately, this isn't as impossible as it sounds.

You can already take some educated guesses based on the profile of your client, the project, and the estimated time required to complete the job. Be careful, however. As Diana Wimbs points out in her book *Freelance Copywriting*, "If you quote too high a fee, you not only risk pricing yourself out of that particular project but also any future work from the same source. Equally, if you put too low a value on your work, clients may be wary about your ability and professionalism."

I usually start the negotiating process by suggesting a price range. In most cases, clients will have a copy of my fee schedule, which I publish in the information kit they receive on my services. So they may already have a good idea of my fee range (assuming they have taken the time to review the fee schedule).

Let's say a client wants me to quote on an Internet direct-mail piece aimed at multimillionaire investors (an assignment I recently completed). She doesn't tell me her budget so I say, "Donna, my fee range for this type of project is $900 to $1,800. Does this fit with your expectations?" If Donna says "Yes," I get more project details and quote accordingly. If Donna says, "Ouch, too high!" then I will try to negotiate a suitable price by saying something like, "Donna, this project sounds very interesting, and I'm sure we can make it successful. Can we find a middle ground that fits both our budgets?"

Sometimes, despite your best efforts to negotiate, you and your client will not be able to agree on a price. In this case, you have little choice but to turn down the assignment. In these situations, I try to be diplomatic, saying something like, "I'm sorry we couldn't agree on a price. Although most clients feel my rates more than pay off in marketing results, I admit my fees are higher than most. Perhaps a good copywriter who charges less would be more suitable for your project."

Confirming the Sale

Once you have discussed a project with a client, determined the deadline, and negotiated the fee, you then need to close the sale. This is a fairly simple process for me. All I do is send the client a completed copy of my two-page quotation/agreement. It is an all-in-one form I use for both quoting and receiving client sign-off on the project details, deliverables, terms, and fee.

When a client receives my quotation/agreement, he or she simply signs it and faxes it back to me. In some cases, clients also send me a copy of their purchase order, but I always insist on getting my quotation/agreement signed as well. I never accept a project from any client without having this form signed.

Sample 10 is an example of a quotation/agreement. You are free to modify this form for your own quotes and agreements. However, please have your lawyer review any form you develop before you put it in use. Do not assume that an adaptation or even a direct copy of my quotation/agreement will sufficiently protect your interests.

Sample 10
QUOTATION/AGREEMENT

Best Graphic Communications   June 16, 20--
123 Yonge Street, Suite 5054
Toronto, ON M9B 4T4

ATT: John Smith

Thanks for considering my services.

Project details

Six-Panel Brochure for New Gizmo

I will generate ideas and concepts and write copy for a six-panel brochure as discussed at our meeting today. The copy I develop for this brochure will be adapted for both NN and Transamerica.

My services will include:

- Reviewing in detail all background materials
- Reviewing in detail any competitor materials available
- Offering suggestions, ideas, concepts, approaches
- Any research, meetings, and interviews required
- All copywriting work
- Any revisions you request
- Coordinating my activities with you and your staff

Project schedule

- I will send a detailed content outline to Leanne by e-mail Friday, June 23, at noon.
- You will provide feedback to me on Monday, June 26, by 3:00 p.m.
- I will e-mail a complete, polished draft of the brochure to Leanne by Thursday, June 29, at noon.

Fee

$1,325 plus applicable taxes. This fee *includes* meetings, minor expenses, research, interviewing, brainstorming, writing, rewriting, revising, editing, and all other work described under "Project details."

Revisions

Should revisions be necessary, I will complete these promptly and at *no additional charge*. This is provided such revisions are assigned within 60 days of your receipt of copy and are not based on a fundamental change in the project.

Expenses

You will *not be charged* for any minor, out-of-pocket expenses required to complete this project — including phone, fax, Internet, e-mail, and courier. In the unlikely event a chargeable expense becomes necessary, you will be notified *in advance* for approval.

Invoicing

An invoice is sent *one week* after your receipt of the *initial* draft, payable net 30 days. If a revision is required after this point, it will be completed promptly and at *no charge*. Should you cancel or place this project on hold for any reason, you will be invoiced for all work completed to date.

Errors and omissions

I will make every effort to ensure copy is free of errors and omissions — including errors in spelling and content — but cannot warrant this. I suggest you review copy thoroughly before committing this project to production.

Computer viruses

I use a current version of McAfee VirusScan and scan all files before sending copy by e-mail or CD-ROM. Although this is robust virus protection, I cannot guarantee files will be virus free.

Copyright

The copyright for any creative concepts and copy I develop shall be automatically transferred to you upon full payment of applicable invoice.

Indemnity

You shall hold me harmless against any liability anywhere in the world, including liability arising from copyright infringement and libel, that results in any way from your use of my copywriting services and counsel on this project. I agree to work with your legal advisor to ensure copy complies with applicable laws and regulations.

I look forward to working with you on this project. If the above meets with your approval, simply sign and fax this letter back to me at 905-555-4567.

Thanks,

Steve Slaunwhite

Steve Slaunwhite

_____

☐ AGREED. Please proceed with this project as quoted.

_____ _____ _____ _____
Authorized Signature   Print name   Date   Purchase Order Number

8
How to Write Copy Your Clients Will Love

Information, tips, tactics, and techniques on writing great advertising and other sales materials could easily fill the pages of this book and more. It's a huge topic. Dozens of books and numerous other resources are available on copywriting in general, and on copywriting for specific projects such as direct mail and websites. (I list many of these on the CD-ROM in the Resources section.)

If you're serious about building your copywriting muscle — and you must be to succeed in this business — then I suggest you become a student. All the successful self-employed copywriters I've spoken with are voracious readers on the topic and continually learn all they can. You should, too.

This chapter outlines what I and other experts have learned about writing successful copy for client projects. It's not definitive,

Read all you can on the subject of writing copy. I have never read a book on copywriting, no matter how basic, without learning something new.

but it does represent a good overview of the topic. Follow these simple guidelines and you'll be well on your way to writing copy your clients will love.

Three Questions to Ask before You Write

There are countless examples of copywriting that is wonderful to read. The grammar is impeccable. The phrases are inventive. The words sing. But does that mean the resultant sales letter, direct-mail package, web page, or ad will meet objectives?

The answer, of course, is no.

Good writing alone is not enough to engage the hearts and minds (and wallets) of customers. If that's all it took, a lot of struggling literary authors would be making a lot more money!

So how do you ensure that the marketing piece you're writing isn't just pretty prose? Here are three questions to ask before you tackle any copywriting task:

1. Ask: "What is the goal?"

Exactly what is it that your client wants to accomplish? Do they want an e-mail that encourages HR managers to download a valuable white paper? Or a direct-mail package that motivates gold investors to spend $600 for a newsletter? Or a brochure that helps sales people explain new product features? Be as specific as you can be.

Effective copy is copy that sells, or persuades you to take the next step in the buying process.

It's amazing how many direct-mail and e-mail promotions, and especially general marketing communications, seem to have no clear raison d'être. Don't risk producing something that merely contributes to the clutter. Have a goal, and keep it front and center as you write. You might even want to sticky-note the goal to your computer (as I sometimes do).

2. Ask: "What's in it for the reader?"

Perhaps the biggest mistake that copywriters make is focusing too heavily on the product. This admonition may come as a surprise for some. After all, isn't the product the subject?

Actually, no. The subject is the *customer*. Or, more specifically, the customer's needs, wants, and interests. That means your marketing piece must clearly answer the question every reader asks: "What's in it for me?"

If you focus purely on the product — no matter how revolutionary or value-packed it may be — you risk producing nothing more than a "brag and boast" document. And you know what happens to those. (Waste bin basketball, anyone?)

3. Ask: "What do I want the reader to do?"

Do you want the reader to visit a web page and fill out a form? Do you want them to call a toll-free number and order your product? Perhaps you want potential customers to be prepared (i.e., "watch your mail") because something interesting is going to happen next.

Marketing writing in all its various forms — direct mail, advertising, PR, online — is essentially an exercise in persuasion. Whether it's an obvious "Call Now!", or conveyed merely in the subtext, you must communicate what it is you want the reader to do. If you don't, your copywriting will be like a ship without a rudder. It may look good, but it's going nowhere.

Unlocking the Secrets of Great Copy

Have you ever read a great sales letter, brochure, or website and thought, "This is terrific. How did the writer do it?" Or perhaps you've been persuaded to act by a well-constructed advertisement or direct-mail package. You found yourself compelled to check the "Yes" box and return the reply card, or call the toll-free number and place an order.

Effective copy doesn't happen by accident. It isn't the result of clever wordplays or in-your-face graphics. It is developed from proven, tested techniques that have been honed by advertising copywriters over the decades. Early copywriters, like the great John Cables, blazed the trail that latter-day scribes like you and I follow. The strange thing is, very few writers are familiar with these methods. Many of them guess, trying to be "creative," or think a captivating, intelligent, literary writing style will save the day and make the sale. (It won't.) Don't make this mistake.

Study successful advertisements and direct mail and you'll discover they have certain traits in common. Learn these and you'll never read an ad or brochure the same way again.

Do all great marketing documents have these same characteristics? No. Copywriting isn't an exact science. There are exceptions to

John Caples was a pioneer in direct-response print advertising. One ad he wrote, *"They laughed when I sat down at the piano ...,"* ran successfully for more than 50 years. Caples wrote one of the first books on copywriting, *Tested Advertising Methods*, which is still in print today.

In his legendary book, *Tested Advertising Methods*, author John Caples says, "If the headline of an advertisement is poor, the best copywriters in the world can't write copy that will sell the goods. They haven't a chance. Because if the headline is poor, the copy will not be read."

these rules, which is what makes copywriting so interesting. However, most successful ads and marketing pieces are aligned with the keys outlined in the following sections, and you're taking a big risk by veering too far off this well-paved road.

Gain attention

From the time a consumer gets up in the morning, reads the newspaper with his or her coffee and toast, checks out the weather on TV, and drives into work listening to the radio and passing roadside billboards, he or she is bombarded with dozens of marketing messages. Some of these will have an impact on the consumer, but most will not. Consider how many of the commercials and brochures you see each day that you remember at the end of the day: One? Three? None? In marketing communications, the competition for the hearts and minds of consumers and business buyers is stiff. This is why it's so important that your copy break through the clutter and gain attention. If it doesn't, no matter how well written it is, the piece is doomed.

The headline

Since words are a copywriter's building blocks, you must use words to gain attention. The best place to begin is with the headline. Studies in print advertising show that readers respond to an advertisement more because of the headline than any other element in the ad, including design elements. No matter how flashy the images, or how compelling the body copy, headlines are the real workhorse. Some copywriters have been able to increase response by up to 400 percent simply by tinkering with a headline. Rarely can this be accomplished by rewriting the body copy or altering the visual.

Headlines don't exist just in ads. All marketing communications begin with a headline of some sort. In a brochure, it's the words on the cover. On a website, it's the main header on the home page. In a sales letter, it's the first sentence (although many sales letters do use traditional headlines, called overlines).

How do you write a great headline? There are numerous approaches, but the fail-safe method is to focus on the main benefit of the product or service and connect it with the target audience. If you're writing about a new model of car and appealing to sports car enthusiasts, focus the headline on speed or the car's sexy shape.

If you're writing about banking services and the target is small-business owners, focus on the timesaving, money-management benefits. If the product has a benefit that is head and shoulders above the competition (such as a dramatically lower price or an enticing free offer), you might decide to make this the focus of the headline. Headlines that appeal to the reader's self-interest have a good chance of gaining attention.

Of course, there are plenty of other ways to brainstorm effective headlines. A good way to learn how to write them well is to study others. Review the magazines, brochures, and direct mail that come your way and look for ads that successfully gain attention and pull the reader into the sales message. Look particularly for ads that you see repeatedly and direct mail you receive over and over again — these are the proven performers. Study how the headlines are constructed. Make lists (such as the one in Sample 11) and you'll soon develop a repertoire of methods for creating winning headlines.

Visuals

If the headline is the workhorse of marketing materials, where do visuals fit in? Don't they also do a lot of the work in gaining attention? Absolutely, and, although visuals are the domain of the art director, graphic designer, or illustrator, copywriters also contribute to visual ideas and concepts. I once wrote a headline that said, "Plug this … into that … and breathe easy. Your network is now protected." It was a direct-mail piece for an automatic backup system designed to protect computer data. But it wouldn't have made sense without the visual. The visual showed an IT manager plugging the unit into the network, demonstrating how easily and quickly the system can be installed and working. So if you have an idea for a visual that can add punch to your marketing document, suggest it.

Presentation

The overall concept and presentation of a marketing document can also gain attention. For example, in business-to-business direct mail, dimensional mailings are popular (although very expensive). Most direct mail is flat — a letter, a reply card, a brochure — and is mailed in an envelope. Dimensional mailings, however, are three dimensional and are mailed as a package, not in an envelope. For example, a California-based cookbook publisher mailed a single, personalized oven mitt to a select list of prospects. (If you wanted the matching second mitt, you had to order the cookbooks!)

Sample 11
34 WAYS TO WRITE A HEADLINE

1. **Tell a story:**
   They laughed when I sat down at the piano but when I began to play!
      (Famous ad that sold correspondence piano lessons for more than 50 years.)

2. **Appeal directly to the reader's self-interest:**
   Want a bigger share of the pie?
      (Brochure targeted at insurance brokers promoting the sale of segregated funds.)

3. **Begin with "How to":**
   How to make the world's fastest, easiest-to-learn CAD program pay for itself on the first job.
      (Ad for a free report; part of a two-step selling process.)

4. **Ask the reader if he or she needs the product:**
   Need to know who's who in Canadian marketing?
      (Ad selling a directory of contacts in the Canadian marketing community.)

5. **Offer to save the reader money, time, or both:**
   Here's how to save a bundle off your UPS-carried imports (and save you a lot of work).
      (Direct-mail sales letter for customs brokerage services.)

6. **Address reader skepticism head-on:**
   "You seriously think you can reduce my UPS costs and deliver the highest reliability at the same time?"
      (Headline is in the form of a quotation from the reader. Ad for industrial power management hardware.)

7. **Use an everyday colloquialism:**
   That about wraps it up.
      (Ad for insulating house wrap used by residential builders.)

8. **Make a compelling statement of fact:**
   You've never seen an 80kA surge protector this small.
      (Ad for surge protection.)

Sample 11 — Continued

9. **Give a dire warning:**
Beware of parts unknown.
(Ad promoting the use of OEM manufactured parts only. Fear is a powerful motivator, but if not used carefully you risk alienating the reader.)

10. **Offer a compelling business-building benefit:**
Multiply the response rates of your catalog, website, and e-mail in just 24 hours ...
(Ad for voice broadcasting systems.)

11. **Ask a question:**
If your e-commerce orders double, could your infrastructure handle it?
(Ad for e-commerce software and management services.)

12. **Make an introduction:**
Donnelley introduces ... The most powerful consumer database on the planet.
(Ad for a consumer database.)

13. **Use an actual client testimonial:**
"I wanted the best protection available and APC delivered."
(Ad for power protection. A client testimonial can make a very powerful headline. Trouble is, it can be difficult to get permission to use the headline in an advertisement.)

14. **Distinguish the product from the competition:**
Unlike our competitors, this is not the first device we've made for photographers.
(Print ad for high-resolution color copier.)

15. **Use the word "New":**
A whole new way to use 35MM film!
(Print ad for dual-format film.)

16. **Use the word "Discover":**
Discover the secret of a good night's rest.
(Double coupon mailer for an adjustable bed.)

17. **Announce an award win:**
Awarded Best Lens Around the World.
(Print ad for camera lens including a list of four international awards. Mentioning product awards has also been successfully used in selling software.)

18. Simply say what you do:
Paragon will put your chairs in a row!
   (Ad for meeting-planning services.)

19. Make an offer:
Let's Trade. Send us your business card and we will send you a sleeve of PRECEPT *extra distance golf balls.*
   (Ad for sports shop.)

20. Let the president or CEO do the talking:
"Everyone doing business directly ... to me that's the power of the Internet."
   (Ad featuring a quotation from the president of a major computer manufacturer/seller.)

21. Use a clever play on words:
Out sanding performer.
   (Ad for a sanding power tool.)

22. Ask the reader to see the benefit:
See your room in a whole new light.
   (Ad for wallpaper.)

23. Ask the reader to picture the benefit:
Can you picture your employees' faces when they see how smoothly their move went?
   (Direct-mail for employee relocation services. You can also use the word "imagine" to great effect.)

24. Make a list:
Three good reasons why you should order the new 2005 Thomas Global Register today ...
   (Direct-mail brochure for reference library. Lists are effective; people love to read them.)

25. Give something away free:
This book is invaluable, indispensable ... and it's FREE!
   (Direct-mail sales letter for trade show displays. The book is actually a premium for responding to a "free information" offer.)

26. Tell readers this is their last chance:
Last chance to introduce PaperPort to your OmniPage Pro OCR *Software at reduced pricing!*
   (Internet direct mail selling a software add-on.)

27. Make a claim of superior performance:
Holds wood together better than wood does.
    (Ad for carpenters' glue.)

28. Quote from an authority:
"Fires caused by electrical faults simply can't be prevented."
    Source: 1995 Annual Report of the Canadian Association of Fire Marshals.
    (Ad for arc fault protection technology.)

29. Announce a sale:
William Ashley's Summer Sale. Save up to 60%.
    (Newspaper ad for fine dishware and cutlery.)

30. Put the price in the headline:
Did someone say, White Sale? Only $3,959 while supplies last.
    (Ad for LCD projector.)

31. Says it's the first:
What do you call a true SXGA LCD projector with 3300 ANSI Lumens and a Digital PC Interface?
    The World's First.
    (Ad for digital presentation projector.)

32. Say it's number one:
Presenters' #1 Free-Space Mouse.
    (Ad for handheld mouse for presentations.)

33. State the problem:
So, you have to give a presentation for Sue in San Francisco, Patricia in Paris, and Nick in New York ... and all by tomorrow.
    (Ad for virtual meeting software.)

34. Offer the reader a test:
Pop Quiz
    Which ATM adjustment notice prompted a Reg E dispute?
    (Ad for an image-based ATM balancing system.)

I recently worked on a mailing for a major computer manufacturer aimed at the reseller market. This target group is highly sales oriented and constantly looking for ways to increase business. So we mailed them a sales guide enclosed within a nugget of gold (not real gold, of course). Now, if you were a money-motivated reseller, wouldn't a nugget of gold get your attention?

Be better than the competition

When clients ask me how I will begin their copywriting project, I say, "By studying the competition."

Competitor materials give you a convenient benchmark to meet — and exceed. Consumers and business buyers alike are natural comparison shoppers. So, when crafting marketing copy, you must help to educate buyers on how your product or service stacks up against the competition.

In advertising, this is referred to as determining a product's unique selling proposition (USP). This is usually the one feature — or sometimes many features — that distinguishes your product from the competition and that has perceived value for the buyer. For example, if you're writing a brochure about a vacuum cleaner, you might be tempted to promote how well it cleans dirt from carpeting. This is a valid point worth mentioning, but unless it sucks dramatically better than other vacuum products, a more effective approach would be to focus on the vacuum's 20-foot hose. This is a feature the competition does not have. So you can say something like, "Clean an entire room without once dragging your vacuum. Our exclusive 20-foot hose means no more back strains!"

Look for legitimate ways to use words and phrases such as "The best ...," "The most ...," "The lowest ...," "The highest ...," "The only ...," "Our exclusive ...," "Our proprietary ...," which all imply product features no one else has. If the product or service you're writing about has a standout, exclusive feature that buyers love and the competition can't touch, put it front and center in your copy.

"But the product I'm writing about isn't much different from the competition!" you say. Sure it is. If you can't find anything distinguishable to boast about, take a closer look at the company selling the product. Does it have a unique approach to servicing customers? Is its money-back guarantee or product warranty better? Is its price lower? Is it more trusted in its target market? Does it offer other complementary products that make it a one-stop shop? Does it have better payment terms and options? Does it cover a wider sales territory (i.e., can it serve multiple locations)?

When I get stuck trying to distinguish a product or service I'm writing about, I ask my client, "If I'm a buyer, why should I buy from you and not your competition?" This question usually yields some useful answers.

Talk benefits

When writing copy that sells and persuades, your main ammunition will be features and benefits. *Features* are those things that describe the product or service you're writing about — what it does and how well it does it. *Benefits* are those things that describe the effect of those features on the buyer — how these will save time, save money, add enjoyment, add prestige, build business, make money, or otherwise make the buyer's life or business better. For example, you may not care if the new stereo you just purchased has the latest in audiophonic circuitry — you just want to get it home and listen to the great-sounding music it plays. The audiophonic circuitry is the feature. The great-sounding music you enjoy is the benefit.

Features are those things that describe the product or service you're writing about. Benefits are those things that describe the effect of those features on the buyer.

When copywriting, it's not always easy to discern what is a feature and what is a benefit. What looks like a benefit may really be a feature in disguise. For example, let's say you're writing a brochure for a new mutual fund, and you learn that the fund has a five-year track record of a 23 percent return with only moderate risk. Sounds like a great benefit. But is it? The fact is, the 23 percent return is really just a feature. To make the story complete, you must spin this feature into a benefit the reader can understand and identify with. For example, you might write:

> *"... relatively high return with only moderate risk means you'll be achieving your retirement goals sooner, without worrying as much about the ebbs and flows of the market."*

Benefits — whether they concern saving time and money or promoting enjoyment and satisfaction — ultimately concern how the buyer will feel after making the purchase. There's an old saying in the sales profession: "People buy on emotion, and justify with logic." So illustrating the benefits helps to get the reader emotionally involved.

Support your claims with specifics

Consumers and business buyers today tend to be skeptical, and are wary of broad, vague, and unsubstantiated claims. They say, "Prove it." And, as a copywriter, this is your job.

But you'll find it isn't always easy to get specifics. I recently worked with a client in the business services sector who was advertising the business' low rates. Only after a lot of probing was I able to determine that their rates were actually at least 15 percent lower than their competitors' rates. Now, which is more persuasive? "Enjoy our low rates" or "Enjoy rates at least 15 percent lower than your current broker?"

Whenever you're faced with a vague or fuzzy benefit, always dig for specifics. If the product or service you're writing about saves money, how much money? If it saves time, how much time? If it improves your golf swing, by what percentage on average? Don't say, "Our dunnage bags cut skid unitization costs." Say instead, "Our dunnage bags cut skid unitization costs by up to 23 percent." Use numbers, measurements, percentages, charts, graphs, comparisons, tables, and other copy structures that say to the reader: "We're not just boasting. We can prove these benefits."

What do you do if you can't get specifics on a product benefit? When I'm faced with this challenge, I use a technique I call "Imagine." I say something like, "Imagine if your shipping company could also customs clear your imports at the border. Imagine how much time this would save." This approach engages readers' imaginations in the selling process, and this can be very powerful and persuasive.

Use endorsements

Nothing adds credibility to a marketing document more than a third-party endorsement. This can be from a current satisfied customer, but can also be a product review in a trade magazine, a nod of support from an industry association, or an endorsement from a leading expert, industry authority, or celebrity.

If you're fortunate enough to have a third-party endorsement at your disposal, don't bury it in the copy. I'm amazed at how many brochures, websites, and other sales documents put client testimonials near the end. Put them front and center! They pack a powerful sales punch.

Explain features; sell benefits.

Specifics sell. Instead of saying something vague and meaningless, such as, "We're dedicated to superior service," say instead, "Our service department has a 95 percent same-day response record."

If you don't have actual third-party endorsements, you can create a similar effect by highlighting the market acceptance of the product or service — or using the "implied endorsement." I recently wrote a direct-mail package for a software product that had a successful new product launch. The headline read:

The results are in! Engineers nationwide are raving about EdgeWare Dynamo!

The headline was true; engineers were raving. The copy went on to describe client reaction and acceptance of the product, although no actual client testimonials were given.

You can also use phrases that state a market position:

Recommended #1 by doctors nationwide;

Or imply a market preference:

Where do private investors turn when they need news they can use?

These suggest third party endorsements when you don't have an actual testimonial on hand. (Just ensure the claims you make are true.)

Reduce the risk

Making a buying decision is a difficult step for anybody. As a consumer, you're worried about paying too much or not receiving the benefits promised. If you're a business buyer, you may be concerned with how a purchase will affect your reputation and career. No one has climbed the corporate ladder by gaining infamy for making a dumb buying decision.

Even when a buyer is sold on the product benefits, getting over the hump of actually making the purchase can be difficult. After all, what if the product or service doesn't live up to its promise? I once purchased a small vacuum that claimed it was the home version of those more powerful shop vacuums used in industrial settings. Just what I was looking for! But when I got it home and tried it out, it was awful. The thing wouldn't function properly, even on the simplest of jobs. When I returned it to the store for a refund, I was told it had no manufacturer's guarantee. I was stuck with the vacuum. I felt taken.

"There is nothing like a positive quote from a third party to enhance the believability of what your materials say about your product or company," writes Janice King in her book *Writing High-Tech Copy That Sells.* If it's possible to include a third party endorsement, work it into the marketing document you're writing.

When structuring your copy, always look for ways to lower the risk for the reader.

The money-back guarantee is probably the most common, and most effective, risk-reducing device used in copywriting. Buyers say, "What have I got to lose? If I don't like it, I get my money back!" My wife recently received a direct-mail package for a large reference book that offered a money-back guarantee. It even included packaging materials and postage to further reduce the hassles of returning the book if she wasn't satisfied. How's that for reducing buying jitters!

If you can't offer a money-back guarantee, then try some other way to lower the risk of buying. You might write that technical service for the product is free for 90 days. Or that the company will provide implementation assistance for up to a year. Or that installation is free (the thought here is that if the company is going to install the product, they are going to make it work properly).

You can also refer to the product's track record as a way to reduce risk:

The reference manual pharmacists have trusted since 1919.

This headline suggests the reference manual has been published and accepted for so long that it must be good.

Include a call to action

During my early sales career, a sales manager told me, "Steve, there are three keys to successful selling:

1. Ask for the order.

2. Ask for the order.

3. Ask for the order."

I took his advice to heart.

In direct response marketing, like direct mail, a call to action is a necessity. Don't leave a prospect guessing what to do next. You must include clear instructions to the reader to respond to your marketing message. In fact, I believe all marketing communications, whether a brochure, website, sales letter, or ad, must ask the reader to take the next step in the sales cycle. This could mean placing an order, agreeing to a meeting, or considering a trial offer.

Your call to action can be very direct and specific:

Return this reply form today for your FREE trial subscription ...

Or more general:

Please call us any time for more information.

In his *Weekly Copywriting Tips* sent by e-mail to subscribers, copywriter Alan Sharpe offers the following tips for creating a strong call to action:

- Give a deadline for ordering
- Warn of a price increase
- Establish a trial or introductory period
- Offer a gift or premium
- Offer a free sample
- Offer a no risk trial
- Offer an "unadvertised special" or "secret offer"
- Use "not available in stores"
- Offer an upgrade
- Throw in supplies

Specialized Copywriting Tasks

Although we go into individual types of projects in detail in the next chapter, there are unique branches of copywriting that require special attention.

Writing for the Web

Easily the fastest-growing market for self-employed copywriters is the World Wide Web. Think about it. Just a little more than a decade ago you could count the number of web pages on the Internet using a jar of pennies. Today that would be impossible. According to the search engine Google, there are more than 8 billion web pages online. Now that's a lot of pennies!

Writing for the Internet has emerged as a huge market for freelance copywriting services. Clients need copy that drives more traffic to their websites and entices customers to click, explore, download, and buy.

E-commerce websites, which sell goods online, are the fastest growing type of business in the world. These businesses are looking for every competitive edge they can find in their quest for online customers. According to Nick Usborne, an online copy expert and author of *Net Words*, "Go to your favorite website, strip away the glamour of the design and technology and you're left with words … words are your last, best way to differentiate yourself online."

More and more website owners are realizing that it takes great copy to make sales online. So they are increasingly looking for copywriters to craft web pages, microsites, landing pages, e-mail, and more.

You can do well financially by writing online. In fact, some copywriters specialize exclusively in this market. The next chapter will provide you with tips on how to write effective copy for the most common online projects.

Writing "long copy" sales letters

You've seen them in the mail, and on the Internet. Those mammoth sales letters that run on for pages, or scroll down your computer screen for what seems to be a vertical mile. Do people really read these things?

Obviously, they do — or else marketers wouldn't spend time and money creating these unique and often controversial promotions.

Long-copy sales letters are nothing new. Since the early days of direct mail, more than a century ago, long letters have been written to sell everything from magazine subscriptions to trips around the world. In fact, a multipage sales letter was the norm during most of the history of direct marketing.

These days, however, long-copy letters are less common. That's mainly because there are far fewer "readers," thanks to television and video games. Still, these types of letters are being used extensively in the promotion of paid-subscription newsletters and other "information products" and, recently, in the fast-growing natural remedies industry.

Very few copywriters have mastered the style and techniques required to hold the attention of a reader for twelve pages and more. It takes training, experience, and a bit of a knack.

If you do decide to pursue long-letter copywriting assignments, the income potential is attractive. Not only can you earn a high fee per assignment — in some cases $6,000 and more — you can also receive commissions should your sales letter become "the control." In some cases, commissions can add up to tens of thousands of dollars.

In addition to the copywriting tips listed earlier in this chapter, here are some additional points specific to long-copy sales letters.

A "control" is a direct-mail letter that is so successful, no other letter tested against it has beaten it.

- *Make a big promise up front.* Some of the most successful long-copy letters work because they make an almost unbelievable claim up front — often in the headline. Make sure it's specific. Vague, empty promises such as "Double Your Income!" don't work.

- *Write a great lead.* The lead consists of the headline and opening few paragraphs of your letter. It's crucial that this section captivates readers and motivates them to stay with you through the rest of the letter.

- *Create vivid "word pictures":* Because of its length, a long-copy letter gives you plenty of room to create scenarios, illustrations, examples, and stories with your words. Take advantage of this. Put the reader in your pictures!

- *Use subheads effectively.* Ideally, the reader should be able to get the gist of the message, the benefits, and the offer just by skimming the subheads. And many readers will do just that.

- *Write in a conversational style.* Make your letter sound like it's from a living, breathing human being. Avoid using a stilted, formal tone.

- *Build belief.* Prove your claims throughout with testimonials, reviews, and statistics. Constantly demonstrate credibility and sincerity. Quote experts.

- *Make every paragraph count.* Write a lazy, dull paragraph and you'll lose the reader — and, subsequently, the sale. Each paragraph has to say something fresh and meaningful, and in an interesting way.

Business-to-business, or B2B, refers to companies that sell products and services to other businesses.

- *Don't be afraid to use fear.* Remind the reader of the consequences of *not* buying. This may seem hard-sell, and it is. But that's the nature of long-copy letters. Soft sell doesn't work here.

- *Summarize the benefits at the end.* Some readers will skip to the end of the letter. Others will forget certain benefits highlighted elsewhere.

There are dozens of other tricks of the trade for writing this unique brand of promotion. If you're interested in pursuing long-letter projects, consult the Resources section on the enclosed CD-ROM for books and courses available.

Writing for the B2B market

A few weeks ago I received a call from a marketing manager of a seminar company. She was obviously frustrated. Her e-mail promotion of a leadership seminar had failed miserably. Time was running out before the event date. She needed answers fast. So she asked if I could review the piece and get back to her with recommendations.

Once I had read the promotion, I immediately recognized the mistake. Although it was a well-crafted piece of copywriting, it spoke to the audience as if they were consumers shopping for car insurance. There was little in the text that would appeal to the serious-minded, results-driven business executive.

Fortunately, I was able to rewrite the copy and, as a result, her next promotion was a huge success.

There are plenty of similarities between consumer and business-to-business copywriting, but there are a lot of differences as well. Copywriters who fail to respect these differences do so at their peril.

Here are some top tips for writing powerful B2B copy:

- *First, stress the* personal *benefits.* Business buyers are individuals. So explain how your product will save them time, make their job easier, make them look good to their superiors, get them promoted, advance their career, get them home by five.

- *Then, stress the* business *benefits.* Business buyers act on behalf of a company. So highlight how your product will reduce costs, increase revenues, avoid liabilities, gain a competitive advantage, improve quality, boost productivity, accelerate cash flow.

- *Features are important too.* Don't rely on benefits alone to sell to a business audience. You must explain all the features fully. A human resources manager will want to know the dry research statistics behind a new training program. An engineer will need the technical specs before he orders a new pump bearing.

- *Write to the job title.* Not all business buyers have the same beliefs, interests, and desires — all information you need to know to sell your target audience. For example, a financial manager will have very different purchasing habits than a sales manager. The first will want to keep costs down and buy only if you demonstrate a solid payback. The second, by contrast, may be willing to spend just about anything to reach his or her sales targets.

- *Demonstrate a specific need.* A consumer may buy a product simply because he or she likes or enjoys it. A business buyer, however, will only make a purchase if the business actually needs the product. There's no bluffing your way through it. Your copy must present a solid "business case." If available, use specific return on investment (ROI) data and payback statistics.

- *Highlight the track record.* Unlike consumers, business buyers don't want to be the first to try something. Instead, they want products and services that are already working well at other companies. So be sure to include plenty of customer testimonials, product reviews, client lists, case studies — anything that establishes a track record of success.

- *Get to the point quickly.* The main challenge in B2B is to write short, effective chunks of copy. Business buyers have no patience for rambling text or long-winded lead-ins. They're too busy! So you must quickly explain what your product is, what it does, and how it benefits — otherwise the business buyer will simply click away.

- *Speak their language.* Every profession has its own buzzwords, acronyms, and colloquialisms. So if you're writing online copy aimed at IT managers, for example, be sure to use phraseology they are familiar with. **Tip**: Review the trade publications your audience reads to get a sense of the language. **Warning**: Be accurate. Nothing will torpedo the credibility of your copy more quickly than incorrectly using a familiar term.

Some copywriters are intimidated by business-to-business products because these tend to be more complex and technical. This is true of many, but not all, B2B industries. For example, office supplies are not that complicated. But ERP software is. How do you get your head around technical products so you can write about them effectively? Read about a five-point strategy that will help in Sample 12.

The Best Way to Improve Your Copywriting

Want to know an inside secret to help you improve your copywriting? Here it is. The next time you receive a sales letter or brochure, or read an ad you feel is particularly effective, sit down at your computer and retype it. Actually type word-for-word the copy as written. Don't change anything. Just type.

As you type, you'll learn firsthand how the copywriter has used and organized the words, phrases, and sentences to the best effect. Writing this out is much better, in fact, than anything you can ever learn by just reading. In a sense, you'll be reliving the copywriter's experience. You'll quickly develop a feel for how the copy looks — in terms of length and structure — on your computer screen.

I do this a few times each week, and the process really helps to improve how I write. I'm not completely sure why it works so well. I just know it does. Try it!

Sample 12
FIVE-POINT STRATEGY FOR UNDERSTANDING ANY B2B PRODUCT

1. Read everything.

Ask your clients to send you previous sales literature, web pages, ads, e-mail promotions, letters, user guides, etc. Provide them with a checklist of what you need. Read everything, even if you don't fully understand the terminology. You'll be surprised at how much you'll absorb.

2. Get the glossary.

There's a dictionary available for just about every conceivable topic. I once found an online glossary of snowboarding terms. In fact, online is a good place to start. Type in the industry or product type in a search engine such as Google, then add the word "glossary." Chances are, a number of free options will come up.

3. Buy the children's book.

I got this idea from Steve Manning, an author's coach. Want to learn about semiconductors? Don't buy the grown-up's version of the book. Get the fully illustrated children's book version instead, complete with pop-ups! Your learning curve will be much easier to climb.

4. Ask a sales person.

As a copywriter, you'll most often be dealing with a marketing manager. But who knows the products and customers better than anyone? The people who have to explain it every day, the sales people. So arrange to speak with one or two of these folks.

5. Get pictures.

They are worth a thousand words. Confused about how wicket values are installed in a hydroelectric turbine application? So was I, until I saw some pictures. Ask for them.

9
How to Complete Common Copywriting Tasks

It's impossible to list all the different types of projects you'll encounter in your copywriting business. Just when I think I have tackled them all, a client challenges me with something new. For example, I recently completed a business-to-business telemarketing script for a team of professional sales representatives. Since these professionals approach sales scripts with varying degrees of resistance, this was a particularly challenging project.

So what kind of work can you expect to attract as a self-employed copywriter? Will you be writing the next great catchphrase for Coca-Cola? Creating new adventures for the Energizer

Bunny? Scripting a TV commercial that plays for $2 million a minute on the next Super Bowl? Maybe. But I doubt it.

Glitzy consumer brands are usually handled by elite creative teams at large advertising agencies. Few freelance copywriters get assignments to write television commercials. (I've written exactly one.)

This chapter contains the most common copywriting tasks you'll receive from clients, and offers tips on how to best handle them.

Brochures and Other Sales Literature

There is nothing more ubiquitous in marketing communications than the brochure. It explains, educates, and sells; it is used as an aid during sales calls; it is used as a leave-behind after sales calls; it is mailed to fulfill sales inquiries; it is used as an enclosure in direct mail; it is handed out at trade shows; and it is included in press kits. Most buyers expect to find much, if not all, they need to know about a particular product or service in the brochure.

Brochures come in an astonishing array of sizes, shapes, and folds, from the basic "slim Jim" six-panel, to multipage, saddle-stitched tomes that approach book length.

Oddly, *writing* the brochure will not be your most difficult task as a copywriter. Your most difficult task will be organizing the information, and there are endless ways to do this. Which key messages should come first? What order should they be presented in? Which key messages should be grouped together?

When I write a product brochure, I like to start with a very short, succinct product description and then lead immediately into the most important and compelling benefit. Then I use headlines, subheads, callouts, and sidebars to break up and organize the copy in the most persuasive and captivating manner possible.

If I'm writing a brochure to be used primarily as a sales aid, I imagine myself as a sales rep sitting across the desk from a potential client. I ask myself, "Which benefits would I talk about first? What objections am I likely to face? How can I best overcome them?" Then I organize the information in the same way as I would a sales presentation.

Here's an example of brochure copy that makes good use of benefits backed up by specifics to make a persuasive case:

An incredible 95 percent day-one release record

Fast. That's the best word to describe how ABC Brokerage will steer your shipments through customs. Our leading-edge software systems and electronic link with US Customs combine to give us the earliest possible start on customs processing. The result is minimal delays at the border, meaning your shipments arrive where needed, sooner.

Sometimes brochures are designed to be more educational than sales oriented. For example, technical brochures are expected to provide clearly written product overviews and technical specifications. In these cases, I organize the brochure so the reader can easily glean what he or she needs to know. I include as much specific information as possible, and provide clear explanations and descriptions.

Here's an example of educational content from a financial services brochure. Note the headline written in the form of a question from the reader:

"Okay, so just what is a Seg Fund?"

There's nothing mysterious about Seg Funds. They're simply investment funds held within an insurance contract. They're managed just like mutual funds. But because of the insurance contract, Seg Funds provide you with unique advantages and protection.

Perhaps the biggest mistake copywriters make when writing brochures is forgetting to include important information. It's surprisingly easy to forget the obvious. I once rewrote a brochure my client pulled from distribution because the original copywriter neglected to include one crucial product detail: the weight (an important point to consider before purchasing a roof-top industrial scrubber). Another brochure I recently received in the mail did not have any company contact information, not even a phone number. There was an empty spot on the back, presumably for distributor contact information, but this was missing. Who was I supposed to call if I was interested in this product?

Some clients will expect you to develop ad concepts. This is usually two or three headlines with corresponding ideas for visuals. Since it takes almost as much work to develop three concepts for one ad as it does to write three separate ads, I suggest you charge accordingly.

Advertising

Print ads are relatively easy to write because most follow a classic, proven formula: a headline, a visual, the body copy, and the contact information. There are, of course, variations on this approach.

Some advertisements contain only a visual. I recently came across an ad for a wallpaper manufacturer promoting their upscale line of wallpaper. There was no headline or body copy, just a picture of an origami elephant made with elegantly designed wallpaper. The ad simply read, "York Wallpaper & Fabrics."

Some ads succeed with just a headline and visual and no body copy. This is especially true of roadside billboards and smaller space print ads:

> *Is this your home? It could be ...*
> (Print ad with a picture selling prefabricated log homes.)

Internet banner ads work with only a short headline to persuade a web surfer to click through to the advertiser's home page:

> *Get $2,000 cash back ... on the purchase of any new 2000 model* SILHOUETTE. *Click here for details.*
> (Internet banner ad for the Oldsmobile Silhouette.)

If you receive an assignment to write a print advertisement, focus on developing a strong headline. Many more readers will notice and react to the headline of an ad than will ever read the body copy. This doesn't mean you should ignore the body copy. The body copy, in fact, works hard to make the sale. But this is after the ad has succeeded in gaining the reader's attention and prompting him or her to read further. See Chapter 8 for more on writing effective headlines.

Direct Mail

Direct mail is perhaps the most involving — and lucrative — copywriting assignment you can receive. Famous copywriters have built their reputations based on their success in conceiving and writing direct-mail packages. This is because the effectiveness of a direct-mail piece is measured by the response it receives: sign-ups, new subscriptions, donations, calls to a toll-free number, hits on a web page, business reply cards returned. When your direct-mail package is printed and mailed, the results are inarguable. Your copy either works, or it doesn't. So tackling a direct-mail project can be both tantalizing and intimidating.

There are three basic kinds of direct mail:

1. *Self-mailers.* As the name implies, these do not require an envelope. Postcards are self-mailers. So are folded brochures and flyers that are mailed on their own.

2. *Envelope mailers.* These may contain a letter, coupon, reply card, brochure, and other inserts.

3. *3-D mailers.* These tend to be elaborate mailers, often contained in a box. The contents could be virtually anything. One 3-D mailer I helped create for Hewlett-Packard actually had a faux gold bar inside!

The cornerstone of most direct-mail packages is the sales letter. Master this, and you're well on your way to developing a successful package — no matter what form it takes. In fact, some of the most successful direct-mail packages in history have consisted of a letter and little else.

The sales letter is a challenging component of direct mail. Most copywriters admit to spending more time on the letter than any other part of the package. But the fact is, it's a letter. Most of us write letters, so you shouldn't feel too worried about crafting a successful one. Just relax and write it as if you're writing to a friend or colleague (a friend who is, of course, a member of your target market).

Here are some guidelines to follow that will help you write a successful sales letter:

- *Use "I," not "we."* The sales letter is one person's statement, not a committee's.

- *Write to one person.* This means using words such as "you" and "your."

- *Write in a friendly, conversational tone.* Don't write a sales letter in the same way you write other marketing documents. Forget the "brochure speak." Write as if you're writing to a friend, colleague, or valued customer.

"Remember the following three points ... If you can write a letter that doesn't violate these three little elements, you're home free.

1. The letter should be a single coherent statement.

2. The letter should get to the point.

3. The letter should tell the reader what to do."

— Herschell Gordon Lewis, *Sales Letters That Sizzle*

- *Keep your paragraphs short.* No one wants to plow through a long-winded section of a letter. A good rule of thumb: Don't let any paragraph be longer than seven lines.

- *Use hanging indents and bullet points.* These can help promote readability, highlight the offer, and simplify complex information.

- *Stick to one purpose.* Your reason for writing the letter to the reader should be specific. Don't ramble. Stick to one clear selling message. Remember, you're writing a letter, not a catalog.

- *Get to the point quickly.* Forget warming up, or setting up your reader. Tell him or her why you're writing as quickly as possible, ideally before the end of the first paragraph. A good test: After your first draft, delete your opening paragraph and see if your letter improves (in many cases, it will).

- *Tell the reader what to do next.* This is the call to action, and every sales letter must have one. After you've made your pitch, you have to tell the reader as simply and clearly as possible what he or she must do: Complete the reply card, fax the form, phone this number, etc. Mal Warwick, a specialist in fundraising copywriting, points out in his book *How to Write Successful Fundraising Letters*, "The 'Ask' (pardon my jargon) shouldn't be an afterthought, tacked onto the end of a letter: it's your *reason* for writing."

- *Use a P.S. statement.* These draw attention. Studies have shown that people will often read the P.S. statement first before reading any other part of the letter.

Websites

Website copywriting can be challenging because people tend to be more visually oriented when surfing the Internet than they are when flipping through printed materials. Also, most consumer and business buyers check out a website to get specific information, and they expect to find it quickly, without having to wade through too much text. As a copywriter writing for a website, your challenge is to present the information as persuasively and succinctly as possible.

When I write content for a website, I try to avoid text clutter. This means having no more than two or three marketing messages per screen. If I need more room, I create a new link to another page of information (Internet designers call this "layering"). If creating a new link isn't possible, I fall back on other proven techniques for breaking up copy — callouts, sidebars, bullets. In writing for the Internet, you can also use drop-down text boxes that appear only when the mouse pointer crosses their path.

It's important to organize key messages as logically as possible so Internet surfers can quickly find information and return to previously viewed information. Strive to arrange information as intuitively as possible. I once logged onto a website looking for product and service information. To my surprise, I couldn't find the link. A little surfing revealed that the "product and services" section was buried under the corporate information link, not where I expected to find it.

Often, you'll get an assignment to write the content for a website after the architecture and organization have already been established. This can be tough because you'll be restricted in terms of content, copy organization, and copy length. While writing for a website a few months ago, I came up with a great idea I thought would be easy to incorporate. But the webmaster said, "Sorry, everything's been coded. We can't make that change."

If you're brought in at the tail end of a website project, do your best to write the most effective copy you can under the constraints. Focus on making your copy informative, persuasive, to the point, and accessible.

For more information on writing for websites, take a look at *Writing for the Web: Writers' Edition*, another title published by Self-Counsel Press.

E-Mail Marketing

One of the biggest changes to this profession over the past few years is the staggering growth of e-mail marketing. It's huge. In fact, it's hard to find a company that doesn't use this marketing channel in some way.

Companies, as well as nonprofit organizations, are using e-mail to send special offers, newsletters, announcements, catalog updates, service bulletins, seminar invitations, and much more. According to Jupiter Research, spending on e-mail marketing in the United States alone is projected to reach $6.1 billion by 2008.

Guess what? Someone has to write all those promotions!

So what do you do when a client asks *you* to write an e-mail promotion? Don't panic. It's a remarkably straightforward process.

The first thing you need to know is how this type of campaign works. There are basically two parts:

1. The e-mail message that the customer sees in his or her in-box.

2. The special web page (commonly referred to as "the landing page") that comes on-screen when the customer clicks a link within the e-mail to respond to the offer.

In most cases, when a client asks you to "Write us an e-mail promo," you're being asked to write both the e-mail *and* the landing page. In Sample 13 we take a closer look at how to effectively craft both of these.

A word of warning: Spam — which is mass market e-mailing without the recipients' expressed consent — is a huge issue. So the less your e-mail marketing piece looks like spam, the more successful it will tend to be.

Never participate in a spam e-mail campaign yourself. It's illegal and you'll get yourself into a lot of trouble. Besides, there are plenty of legitimate e-mail campaigns that need talented copywriters. You won't go hungry.

Microsites

A microsite — sometimes referred to as a hypersite — is a mini-website that is built around a specific marketing campaign. For example, I recently wrote a direct-mail package for a travel company that was promoting its new hotel in the south of France. In the package, we included a special web address to a "microsite" that contained information on the resort, including a virtual tour. This website was separate from the company's corporate site.

A microsite is typically less than ten pages. The copy is often exciting, motivating, and informative. Microsites usually contain a call-to-action, asking the customer to sign up for a newsletter, download a special report, call a 1-800 number, or make a purchase. In this respect, a microsite is very much like a print direct-mail package.

Sample 13
TIPS FOR WRITING E-MAIL MESSAGES AND LANDING PAGES

Tips for writing the e-mail message:

Pay attention to the subject line. It's important. Often, the subject line can make or break the success of an e-mail campaign. Think about it. If the e-mail doesn't get opened, it doesn't get read. Keep the subject line to within 60 characters; that's about nine words maximum.

Write several subject lines. This gives your client a choice. He may even test two or three of your subjects lines to determine which one performs best.

Be careful using the word "free." Although powerful in print direct mail, the word "free" has diminished currency on the Internet. In fact, it can actually depress response. So consider using a synonym such as "complimentary," "no cost," or "bonus."

Use a headline. I almost always include a powerful headline in my e-mail campaigns because it tends to improve response. Remember, just because the e-mail has been opened doesn't mean it will get read. Your headline must be motivating. There are dozens of proven techniques for writing a powerful headline (see chapter 8).

Make it look like a letter. E-mail is a personal communication media. So use a personal format, approach, and style.

Get to the point. In print sales letters you can build suspense, sometimes over several paragraphs, before providing full details on the offer. But this strategy doesn't work in e-mail. You must get to the point early, ideally within the first few sentences.

State the offer early. If your offer isn't in the headline, be sure to highlight it within the first few sentences. Never force readers to scroll down to find the offer. They won't.

Repeat the offer at the end. It's important to highlight the offer more than once. I write the offer and reply instructions near the top of the e-mail and then repeat these again near the bottom. My favorite spot is the P.S. Statement.

Always say "click here." When people see "click here" within an e-mail, they know exactly what to do.

Keep it to one page. E-mail is primarily a short-copy medium. Few people are willing to scroll through a 1,500-word tome. So keep your e-mail copy to the equivalent of a one-page letter or less. That's about 250–400 words.

Tips for writing the landing page:

Remind them why they clicked. When the landing page opens, the original e-mail message tends to go out of view, along with all the benefits you've written. So repeat these key benefits on the landing page. I've found that doing this within a text box is very effective.

Finish the story. Because of space restrictions, you might not have had room in the e-mail to complete the selling job. Now you do. Use the landing page to add new information and elaborate on features and benefits.

Never leave them guessing. Don't assume that just because there's an order form on the landing page that people will intuitively know what to do. Guide them through the process. Give clear instructions.

When a client asks you to write a microsite, approach it as you would any website project. But keep in mind that you're not just writing to inform. You're crafting online copy that must motivate the customer to take action.

Case Studies

Case studies have become increasingly popular in recent years, especially among businesses that sell complex products and services that are difficult to understand, or put into perspective, with just a brochure.

If you're not familiar with case studies, rest assured I'm not talking about a dry, technical, or scientific document. Cases studies used in marketing are essentially success stories. Typically, they tell the tale of "product meets customer" and how everyone lived happily ever after.

Go to any major software or technology company website and you're bound to find a section that features free case studies, along with "white papers" or other product information. Read a few. It's a great way to learn more about this interesting hybrid of brochure, testimonial, and article.

Readers love a good story and clients know it. That's why they are always looking for copywriters who know how to craft an effective case study.

There really isn't much of a mystery to writing these. Most are two to four pages in length (although I've seen some six pagers), and are usually written in standard feature article format. In fact, they often get reprinted in trade magazines and journals.

Can you write an article? Then you can write a case study.

Having written hundreds over the years, I recommend you follow the format outlined in Sample 14.

Newsletters and E-Zines

These days, companies are publishing newsletters and e-zines (newsletters published online) by the truckload. Why? By placing their products and services within the context of an article, an aura of credibility is created — especially if a testimonial from a satisfied customer is included. Also, customers read articles for interest and

A "white paper" is a document that describes a new technology or methodology. It is often used as a free giveaway in high-tech marketing promotions.

Case studies are also known as case histories or success stories.

Sample 14
THE CASE STUDY WRITING SEQUENCE

When writing a case study, focus on these elements:

1. **Customer**

   In the lead paragraph, focus on the customer, not on the product or company. Gain attention with an interesting lead.

2. **Challenge**

   Next, introduce the problem. What condition was the customer trying to change or improve? If possible, use the customer's own words by using a quotation.

3. **Journey**

   What steps were taken to solve the problem? What other products or services were investigated? Why didn't these work out? Many case study writers skip this section. *Don't* skip it. This is the place in the story where the reader begins to identify and empathize.

4. **Discovery**

   How did the customer find out about you? In an ad? At a trade show? Through a media interview? This section often acts as a bridge to the remainder of the case study.

5. **Solution**

   This is where you have unbridled freedom to pitch your product or service without fear of sounding too promotional. The earlier sections have earned you this right.

6. **Implementation**

   How was your product or service implemented? Was there any downtime or disruption involved? How long was it before it was up and running at 100 percent? Be honest about any problems that arose and how they were resolved. Highlight instances where you went the extra mile to satisfy the customer.

7. Results

How well did your product or service solve your customer's problem? Be as specific as you can here. If possible, use hard numbers such as savings, revenue gains, sales growth, and return on investment. This is another good spot to include a customer quotation. And a great place to summarize and close your story.

Here's an excerpt from a case study that incorporates the above points:

"Worms." "Macro viruses." "Trojan horses." Terms that make your skin crawl. These are just some of the buzzwords used to describe computer viruses — those malicious invaders that can destroy or dangerously alter files, cause critical data to vanish, grind productivity to a halt, and cause entire networks to go down.

Donald McKay, IT manager for ACME ZipEx Systems, will never forget the day a virus attacked his network. "Our whole business crashed. We lost service. We lost data. And, ultimately, we lost customers." The virus was quickly removed, but the havoc it created lingered for months.

McKay was determined never to face such a catastrophe again. So, he began a mission to find the best industrial-strength virus protection available. The solution he eventually selected was EchoBlast Virus Blocker ...

enjoyment, so a marketing message woven into an article can be very effective. After all, who wants to cozy up on a Sunday afternoon with a good brochure?

If your background includes articles for magazines and other publications, this form of marketing writing will be familiar territory. It's also a great way to break into copywriting if you've had no previous experience. It's often easier to convince a prospective client to hire you to write an article for their quarterly newsletter than to trust you with a major marketing piece. Once you've proven your abilities, however, you're on the radar screen for future assignments.

I suggest you approach a newsletter writing assignment as you would a magazine article. Get the facts, organize them in an interesting way, use quotes if available, and write well.

Press/Media Materials

To promote their products and services, marketers will often attempt to attract the interest of the media. A product mention in a trade-magazine print or online article can add a credibility that is almost impossible to attain with ads and brochures.

The press release is the most common form of media communications. It is usually a one- or two-page announcement written in the form of a news article, complete with headline. In fact, some publications will publish a press release verbatim, although most editors will edit or revise the piece or choose not to use the release at all.

Lynn Fenske, a copywriter and editor who has worked both sides of the media fence offers these writing tips:

- *Be newsworthy.* While assessing a story's newsworthiness is often subjective and instinctive, there are guidelines you can use to test its news appeal. Consider whether your story is immediate. Is it close to home? Does it affect many people? Does it have lasting importance? Certainly emphasize what is "new," "better," or "different" about your subject matter by explaining how it affects the reader.

- *Be brief, especially in the headline.* You are writing to appeal to media professionals who specialize in three-word headlines

Some businesses have a set format for their press releases. For example, they may prefer that new product announcements not exceed two paragraphs, or that a boilerplate company profile be included as the last paragraph of every release.

and eight-second sound bites, so keep your message short and concise. Choose your words carefully. Trying to fit the whole story into a headline or writing more than one full page of body copy does not make for a compelling press release.

- *Follow the set format.* Press releases are structured with a specific place and spacing for all components including the headline, release time, dateline, body copy, end marker, and contact information. *Always* follow the format. Put everything in its proper place, on a document that uses or resembles corporate letterhead.

- *Write like a reporter.* Be factual and objective. Answer the five W's and one H: who, what, where, when, why, and how. Always write the release in a third-person voice using simple, precise language. No ten-dollar words or excessive techno-jargon — unless you want to alienate your audience.

- *Include quotes.* Support the facts in the press release with quotations from key personnel or people directly involved in the story. Their commentary helps to personalize the story and give it relevance and perspective.

Press releases are not the only form of communications to editors, journalists, and others in the media. You may also be asked to write product backgrounders, profiles of senior management, and other materials.

Audio/Visual, CD-ROMs, Video, and Multimedia

Because of the advent of new communication technologies — especially CD-ROMs and the Internet — it's almost impossible for a copywriter to avoid getting involved in scriptwriting. This can seem intimidating to those who have dropped their anchor in prose, but it really isn't all that different.

Scriptwriting is writing dialogue and copy that corresponds with moving images. Today's marketing communications use animation, interactivity, and moving images more than ever. It's not uncommon for a website to open with a "flash" sequence — almost like a short movie. As a copywriter, you'll need to learn to work with storyboards and write for these forms of communications.

When writing for audio/visual, your copy will need to work much more closely with the visuals than when writing for print, so you'll need to work closely with the designer.

In print materials, we think in terms of pages or sections when we write copy. In audio/visual, you need to think in sequences. In an interactive CD-ROM I recently completed, for example, the opening sequence displayed information on a hand-held electronic organizer. The next sequence included client testimonials. The third sequence highlighted service benefits. And so it went. I simply treated each sequence as a copy "page" and wrote accordingly.

When writing a script for an electronic presentation of any sort, there's no need to be intimidated by the format. Use the same copywriting principals mentioned in this book, with perhaps a greater focus on telling the story.

Fundraising Letters

A big market for freelance copywriters is the nonprofit sector — especially charities. These organizations often send out fundraising letters, either by mail or e-mail, to raise the funds needed to support their various causes. For example, the America Cancer Society sends out millions of letters each year asking people to become donors.

Many copywriters earn reasonably good fees writing fundraising letters. And there are a few freelance professionals who specialize exclusively in this area.

Working on these types of projects can be rewarding in two ways. First, you can make good money, especially if you establish a track record. Second, you can feel good about the cause your copy is helping to support. My friend Ron Marshak, a copywriter with extensive experience in this sector once remarked, "I recently got a call from a client, a health charity [regarding a direct-mail package I wrote]. They said, 'Thanks Ron. Your copy has saved another life today.'" Now that's got to feel good!

Writing a fundraising letter isn't the same as writing a sales letter. In a sales letter, you're asking someone to exchange their dollars for a specific product or service. In a fundraising letter, you're asking for money and, usually, are not offering anything concrete in return. All you're offering to provide in terms of benefit is good feelings.

There are two types of fundraising appeals: the *acquisition letter* that is sent to people who have no history of donating to the charity; and, the *renewal letter* that is mailed to those who have supported the charity in the past.

If you're interested in writing for the nonprofit sector, the Resources section on the CD-ROM included with this book lists a number of books available. See Sample 15 for five quick tips for writing an effective fundraising letter.

Keeping Your Skills Sharp

The type of projects most typically handled by freelance copywriters have changed tremendously over the past decade — and will remain in flux for the coming years.

When I wrote the first edition of this book, I was doing very few e-mail marketing assignments and I hadn't even heard of the term "microsite." Now I handle dozens of these assignments every year.

What's next? There are advances in using video streaming on websites and in e-mail. There were a lot of false starts in this technology. It was expensive and cumbersome. But because of new innovations, video streaming is making a comeback. Will you and I be writing scripts for these? Only time will tell.

There's a new fad in marketing that is gathering momentum as I write this. It's called "Blogs." In a nutshell, a blog — short for weblog — is an online diary that a company keeps on the web. For example, the president of a cereal company may keep a blog of his thoughts on nutrition and healthy living and customers can respond and add their own opinions.

The jury is out as to whether a blog has any currency in marketing communication. So far, it seems like a whimsical fad. But who knows? I may be asked to ghostwrite a blog for a client someday soon.

How do you stay prepared? The best way I've found is to keep up with your professional education. Read articles and books. Build a network with other copywriters and keep in touch. Keep your skills sharp, and you'll be ready for anything.

Sample 15
FIVE TIPS FOR WRITING A FUNDRAISING LETTER

Here are five quick tips for writing an effective fundraising letter.

1. **Use a friendly, conversational tone.**

    The letter should sound like it's from one person, not a committee. Use "I" and "you." Keep the vocabulary simple.

2. **Be clear.**

    Don't dance around the issue. If the goal is to ask for money, then ask for it. There's no need to soft-pedal the intent of the letter by using the word "support."

3. **Explain what the money will do.**

    Provide specific details as to how the money will be used and what the potential results will be. For example, you could say "… a $50 donation will provide enough vaccine to protect this Sri Lankan village for a year."

4. **Say "Thank You" in advance.**

    Expect that the reader will support the cause. Say thank you early and keep saying it.

5. **Give the reader a reason to send money now.**

    There are many ways to do this. You could use a special date, such as Christmas. Or highlight a current crisis or natural disaster. Or simply illustrate how desperate and time-sensitive the need currently is. The point is to infuse your copy with urgency.

10
Managing Your Work, Time, and Money

An overwhelming majority of self-employed copywriters run a solo operation, so, chances are, you will never have to manage employees. You're on your own. You supervise no one. No one supervises you.

But this doesn't mean you can be a free spirit and cast all thoughts of management aside. In fact, there are three very important things you will have to manage, and manage well, in order to succeed as a freelance copywriter. In fact, how you manage these can mean the difference between a profitable, stimulating business, and a stressful, chaotic one. What are these three things? They are your work, your time, and your money.

Developing good organizational and self-management skills is vital. You'll constantly have to keep these skills sharp to stay sane and successful in this business. If you let your guard down — especially in the area of money — you'll pay the price.

Here are some strategies I and other self-employed professionals use to keep the gears and rollers of our businesses well-oiled and running smoothly.

From Start to Finish: How to Complete a Copywriting Assignment

You've just received an order for an assignment from a client. Congratulations! But don't celebrate too soon. You now have to tackle the assignment — planning, writing, polishing — so you can deliver the completed copy to your client by the deadline. Only then can you send an invoice and wait expectantly for your check.

As a self-employed copywriter, you'll spend the majority of your time working on copywriting assignments. You'll be managing yourself. That's why it's important to develop a set process to follow with each assignment. Working by instinct will get you only so far — sometimes in the wrong direction. Develop a project completion system so you can approach tasks systematically. This takes the sting out of questions like, "Where do I start?" or "Where do I go from here?"

A few years ago, I got tired of approaching each project differently. I felt frustrated because I wasn't building on what I had learned about completing a copywriting task. If someone asked me how I approach a new project, I gave a long, rambling answer. The fact was, I didn't really know.

Now I do. I have developed a four-step process that I follow with every assignment I tackle. This has been very successful for me. No longer do I waste time thinking about how to start a new project, or what to do next if I get stuck midway through. I simply follow the four steps.

I call this step-by-step approach to completing copywriting tasks the CODE method:

C — Collect

O — Organize

D — Draft

E — Edit

The CODE method is great for scheduling. When I receive an assignment, I simply create a timetable based on completing each section of the CODE. This takes a lot of the guesswork out of determining how long a project will take. For example, if I have a new direct-mail project to complete, I might plan to do "C" on Monday, "O" on Tuesday, and so forth.

If at all possible, try to schedule the completion of each component of CODE on separate days. Or, for a very short project, at different times of the same day. For some reason that I don't fully understand, the breaks in between make the writing process smoother and faster, and the resultant quality much higher. When I attempt to do all these stages in one go, with no breaks, the opposite happens. (Although, sometimes, a timeline can be so tight you just don't have any other choice.)

Collect

When you first receive a copywriting assignment, you are going to have to collect a lot of information up front from your client. You'll need to know details on the target market, the features and benefits of the product or service, its characteristics, how the product or service differs from the competition, its strengths, and its weaknesses.

Rarely is this information contained in one neatly organized document. More than likely, your client will present you with a stack of memos, old brochures, competitor materials, creative briefs, data sheets, and other documents. And the information you need to proceed with the project may still be incomplete. You may have to review their website in detail — and competitor's sites as well. You may need to interview product managers, technical managers, and other contacts in your client's organization to fill in the gaps in your information.

Most of the copywriters interviewed for this book say they immerse themselves in all the information they can get their hands on about the product or service they are writing about. I try to learn and understand at least as much as my client does, sometimes more.

But learning all you can about the product is only half the job. You also have to understand the audience your copy will be trying to educate and persuade. Who are they? What do they do? What are

"You need to be like a reporter," explains New York copywriter Randy Rensch. "You have to dig deep to get the complete story."

their responsibilities? What keeps them awake at night? What are their existing beliefs about the product? What are their interests and desires? Too many copywriters make the mistake of focusing too much on the product and too little on the prospect. If you can't close your eyes and imagine taking a walk in their moccasins, you don't know enough about the target audience. Do more research.

Besides reading all the background information the client supplies me, there are two additional things I do to fully understand the target audience. The first is to study the magazines they read. For example, I once wrote a promotion aimed at snowboarding enthusiasts. After reading some of the publications aimed at this market, I not only knew what "Misty flip" meant, I could almost feel it! The second thing I do is speak to some of the salespeople because they deal with the target audience on a day-to-day basis; they can tell you things about what makes these prospects tick that you just can't find out any other way.

Take a look at Sample 16, in which copywriter Bob Bly, no stranger to complex copy tasks for leading business-to-business clients, offers steps for culling the information needed to successfully complete a copywriting assignment.

One of the more important tools I create during this information-gathering process is what I refer to as a master sheet, which includes the following:

- The features and benefits organized in priority

- Characteristics that distinguish the product or service from the competition

- A profile of the target market (so I know who I'm writing to)

- Any specific information that must be included in the piece such as company name, contact information, disclosures, warranties, and disclaimers

A master sheet can end up being a page long, or ten pages long, depending on the product or service involved. But once this is complete, it makes it much easier to write the document. When I need an important nugget of information, it's right there at my fingertips. Sample 17 shows an example of a master sheet I created for a family of segregated funds.

Sample 16
HOW TO PREPARE FOR A COPYWRITING ASSIGNMENT

This sample is excerpted from Bob Bly's online article, "How to Prepare for a Copywriting Assignment," and is reprinted here with his kind permission. Although this article is intended to help clients brief their copywriters, you can follow these points to ensure that you acquire all the information you need to proceed.

Here's a four-step procedure I use to get the information I need to write persuasive, fact-filled copy for my clients.

Step 1: Get all previously published material on the product.

For an existing product, there's a mountain of literature you can send to the copywriter as background information. This material includes:

- Tear sheets of previous ads
- Brochures
- Catalogs
- Article reprints
- Technical papers
- Copies of speeches
- Audio/visual scripts
- Press kits
- Swipe files of competitors' ads and literature

[*Note from Steve Slaunwhite:* I would also suggest you get website addresses (for your client and their competitors), previous sales letters and direct mail, e-mail announcements to customers and prospects, product presentation scripts and slides (these are often PowerPoint presentations), sales scripts and guides, and previous sales proposals.]

Did I hear someone say they can't send me printed material because their product is new? Nonsense. The birth of every new product is accompanied by mounds of paperwork you can give the copywriter. These papers include:

- Internal memos
- Letters of technical information
- Product specifications
- Engineering drawings

- Business and marketing plans

- Reports

- Proposals

By studying this material, the copywriter should have 80 percent of the information he or she needs to write the copy. He or she can get the other 20 percent by picking up the phone and asking questions. Steps 2 to 4 outline the questions to ask about the product, the audience, and the objective of the copy.

Step 2: Ask questions about the product.

- What are its features and benefits? (Make a complete list.)

- Which benefit is the most important?

- How is the product different from the competition's? (Which features are exclusive? Which are better than the competition's?)

- If the product isn't different, what attributes can be stressed that haven't been stressed by the competition?

- What technologies does the product compete against?

- What are the applications of the product?

- What industries can use the product?

- What problems does the product solve in the marketplace?

- How is the product positioned in the marketplace?

- How does the product work?

- How reliable is the product?

- How efficient?

- How economical?

- Who has bought the product and what do they say about it?

- What materials, sizes, and models is it available in?

- How quickly does the manufacturer deliver the product?

- What service and support does the manufacturer offer?

- Is the product guaranteed?

Step 3: Ask questions about your audience.

- Who will buy the product? (What markets is it sold to?)
- What is the customer's main concern? (Price, delivery, performance, reliability, service maintenance, quality, efficiency, etc.)
- What is the character of the buyer?
- What motivates the buyer?
- How many different buying influences must the copy appeal to?

Two tips on getting to know your audience:

- If you are writing an ad, read issues of the magazine in which the ad will appear.
- If you are writing direct mail, find out what mailing lists will be used and study the list descriptions.

Step 4: Determine the objective of your copy.

This objective may be one or more of the following:

- To generate inquiries
- To generate sales
- To answer inquiries
- To qualify prospects
- To transmit product information
- To build brand recognition and preference
- To build company image

Before you write copy, study the product — its features, benefits, past performance, applications, and markets. Digging for the facts will pay off, because in business-to-business advertising, specifics sell.

Sample 17
PRODUCT MASTER SHEET

Client name:

Cross Country Life Assurance
500 Yonge Street
Buffalo, NY 88888
1-800-555-1234
<www.AssurePlus.com>

Product name:

*Assure*PLUS™ family of segregated funds.

Product description:

Family of 11 segregated funds.

Target buyers:

Maturing investors. Those with large retirement savings who are nearing retirement and seeking ways to continue investment growth, but with protections. Age category, 40 plus.

Features and benefits:

Features	Benefits
*Assure*PLUS guarantees 100 percent of your investment.	Peace of mind. Invest in growth funds without fear of losing original investment.
1 free reset each year	Lock in investment gains frequently. Protect your growth.
11 funds ranging from conservative to aggressive growth.	There's a fund that fits your lifestyle, goals, and risk comfort.
All funds are RRSP eligible.	Tax-sheltered growth. Pay less taxes each year you invest. More disposable income to enjoy.
Managed by top investment fund managers with experience managing mutual funds.	Greater growth potential. Earn more money to enjoy during retirement.

Sample 17 — Continued

Features	Benefits
Bypass probate fees.	Relieves your heirs of probate fees. Maintains the value of your estate. Your money goes where you intended it to go. Your family is protected should you unexpectedly die.
Free switches three times each year. If a fund isn't performing as you like, you can switch to another *Assure*PLUS fund.	Don't feel locked in. Save money. Flexibility in knowing you can move your money to a preferred fund any time at no cost.
Easy payment options. You can start investing with just $75 per month.	Easy to know how your funds are doing.
Painless investing. Monthly payments relatively easy to "hide" in most budgets. *Assure*PLUS monthly newsletter, personalized quarterly reports, password-only website access.	Constant, easy-to-read, easy-to-understand information on your *Assure*PLUS investments.

Buyer education (jargon and concepts that need explaining):

What is a segregated or "seg" fund?

They're simply investment funds held within an insurance contract. They're managed just like mutual funds. But unlike mutual funds, seg funds provide you with unique advantages and protection.

About the seg fund guarantee ...

Seg funds guarantee all or part of the money you invest in the plan.

About reset options ...

Seg funds allow you to lock in your investment gains.

How do I invest in a seg fund?

Unlike mutual funds, you have to open a policy. This is because seg funds include a life insurance component, so investors must follow a process similar to buying life insurance (i.e., questionnaire, medical check; if necessary).

Features distinguishing *Assure*PLUS from the competition:

- Most other seg funds offer only a 75 percent guarantee of original investment.
- Many seg funds charge extra for switching between funds.
- Many seg funds don't offer monthly payment plans. Some insist on lump sum investments of at least $1,000.

Disadvantages. Possible reader objections to overcome:

*Assure*PLUS offers only one reset each year. Many other funds offer three or more. Explain that more resets is an "empty" promise by other funds because resets are rarely used more than once each year. We compensate my making our other, more useful benefits more robust.

Things to include:

1. A *comparison chart* between seg funds and mutual funds.
2. A *listing of the 11 funds available*, organized as Conservative Growth, Moderate Growth, and Aggressive Growth. Each fund to include a one- or two-sentence summary of the fund characteristics.
3. A *profile* of the investment management team, written as a "day in the life" story.
4. Explain the *process* of investing in a seg fund. Picture of a seg fund policy.

Copy style:

Informative, conversational, friendly, "plain English." Avoid jargon. Use plenty of "real life" examples with which readers can identify. Explain terms and concepts with clear examples and illustrations.

Call to action:

Ask your financial advisor or insurance broker about *Assure*PLUS Segregated Funds.

Specific information that must be included:

Standard two-paragraph profile of Cross Country Life Assurance provided by the client.

Organize

Once you have collected the information needed to complete the assignment, you must organize the presentation of the information. This will differ based on the type of assignment involved.

For example, if you are creating a website, you'll need to determine what will be on the home page. What links will need to be created? What information will be contained in those links? How will the information be organized on each page?

If you're writing a sales letter, you'll have to decide how the letter will be constructed. Will you use a headline? An envelope teaser? Indents? A "P.S." at the end? How should you open the letter? What is the offer? How will you close the letter on the strongest possible note?

Is this sounding a lot like an outline? Well, in many ways it is. And a lot more …

Once I have decided where the information is going to be placed, I organize the information by creating headlines, subheads, callouts, sidebars, and other copy elements to frame how the key messages will flow. For example, if I'm writing a brochure, I might create a main headline for the cover, and organize the remaining panels with headers and subheads.

During this process I may also develop ideas and suggestions for visuals. If I think a key message will be better presented as a chart or graph, for example, then I will make note. If I develop an idea for a picture or illustration that will work well with a particular headline, I will include this as a suggestion.

By the way, the headlines, subheads, and other titles you write during this Organize stage do not have to be perfect. In fact, they will likely substantially change and evolve before you reach your final draft. But at least now you're getting a clearer picture of how the piece is going to look.

Once I have the headlines, subheads, and other high-level copy elements in place, I do something I call content dumping. This doesn't sound particularly creative, but it's a necessary step. Basically, I use the cut-and-paste features on my word processing software to lift the key messages from the master sheet I created earlier, and paste them under the appropriate headers I have developed.

I compare the organize stage to a painter roughing in a scene with pencil. As the painter does this, a picture slowly emerges from the blank canvas and it becomes clearer and clearer.

In *TurboCharge Your Writing!*, his excellent booklet on writing fast and well, copywriter Joe Vitale suggests, "What you want to do [in the draft] is write without thinking ... don't stop to punctuate or check your spelling or look up a fact. JUST WRITE! ... Ride the wave of enthusiasm that accompanies free-form writing."

What am I left with? I have an organized outline with rough headlines and subheads in place and the content I need for the body copy pasted under each. It's starting to look like a brochure (or website, or direct-mail piece, or whatever I'm writing).

Often, as I'm going through the organize phase of a project — or even if I'm still in the collect phase — I will get the urge to write a sentence, a paragraph, or sometimes a whole section. When this happens, I don't hold back. I go for it. For example, if I'm writing the headline for a letter, I might find myself writing the first few sentences. I never stop this flow just because I'm not yet on the draft step. I let it happen. When I run out of steam, I continue with the organize step until this stage in the process is complete.

Now that I have the project information collected and organized with headers and other structural elements, I'm ready to write the draft.

Draft

For many writers, the draft is the step in the writing process they fear the most. Although you have already completed much of the work in collecting and organizing the information, you haven't actually written any copy yet. This can be terrifying. How are you going to grind all this information into a finished draft?

The fact is, draft is the easiest step of all — and the shortest step. It actually takes me longer to collect and organize a project than it does to write the draft. Think of what you already have on your screen. If you completed "C" and "O" diligently, you already have the headers in place and the content assigned to each. You don't have to think about what to write, or how the information is going to be laid out. You already know. This is what makes the draft step so easy. You just have to write.

I simply look at the content a section at a time, and blast off, writing freely without stopping. I don't care (at this point in the process) how good or bad my writing is. I don't bother to check if words are spelled correctly, or if I'm following the ten thousand or so rules of grammar. I just write.

Regardless of the style I'm trying to adhere to — formal, casual, pedantic, new age, technical — I try to write as conversationally as possible. In fact, I actually visualize a member of the target audience and speak directly to him or her. I find this creates fluid, understandable prose that works best in marketing communications.

You'll find writing easier if you create a mental picture of someone representative of your target market and write directly to him or her. In fact, don't write. Talk. (Just talk with your fingers on the keyboard.)

Ivan Levison, successful at writing Internet direct mail, recently wrote a highly successful e-mail targeted at the young, techno-savvy crowd. In a recent edition of his newsletter, *The Levison Letter*, Levison explains, "When I sat in front of my computer to write this e-mail, I imagined that I was sending a note to a 21-year-old sitting in his messy dorm room."

Once you have a draft written, a lot of the pressure is off. You're nearly there! Now it's time to edit.

Edit

Have you ever read over something you wrote and found yourself mentally editing, correcting, reworking, polishing, and improving sections? We all have. In my experience, most people enjoy rewriting much more than writing. This is because a major obstacle has been eliminated: the blank page (or the blank screen).

Once you've completed the draft stage, a great deal of the stress associated with the project is over. After all, the document is written (although it may not be written well). Donna Baier Stein says that her first draft is always terrible — and she's one of the top direct-mail copywriters in the world! But at least your document is written. Now all you have to do is make it better. And better. And better.

Rewriting and revising is fun. So fun for me, in fact, that I actually offer a service rewriting and revising marketing copy written by others.

As you go through your document over and over again, you'll find yourself polishing sections, fixing paragraphs, rewriting entire sections. You might even change the organization of the piece from what you mapped out during the organize stage. You might discover that a key message you had buried toward the end of a brochure is better presented up front. When this happens, don't be afraid to make the change. There is only one rule to follow during the edit process. Make it the best, most persuasive document possible. Make it work.

Top copywriter Ron Marshak says, "I like deadlines because at least they force me to stop polishing the piece and send it in."

Virtually all assignments I complete are submitted to clients via e-mail. None of my clients ask for a hard copy anymore. There's no reason to. When they receive my copy electronically, they can make changes or comments right on the screen, or send the copy to their designer. No one has to retype the copy.

But you will reach a point when you have to say, "It's finished." This can be harder than you imagine. The fact is, no writing can ever be perfect, no matter how long you tinker with it. And there is such a thing as overwriting to a point where all the personality and flavor of the piece is completely washed out.

When you reach a point during the editing process where you have reworked your copy, scrutinized it, let someone else read it, fixed errors, and now find yourself sitting for long periods sweating over a single word or phrase, you're finished. Sure you could work at it some more and make it a little bit better. But the improvement will be so small as to be virtually unnoticeable, and disproportionate to the hours of extra time you have spent.

Do yourself a favor. Aim for excellence, not perfection. Perfection just doesn't exist.

Submitting the Assignment

Once you have completed the assignment, you need to submit it to your client for review. Sometimes this can be a nail-biting process as you wonder how the client will react to your work. Once you have a few assignments under your belt, however, you'll feel much more confident in your abilities.

I write the client name and title of the project on the top of each page of the assignment and "Prepared by Steve Slaunwhite" with my phone number on the bottom. This way, if someone who doesn't know me is reviewing the copy and has questions, he or she can pick up the phone and ask me.

Also at the top of the page, I date the copy draft. For example, "XYZ Brochure, draft as of July 21." This avoids confusion when the copy and subsequent revisions make the rounds of the client's approval committee.

There is no set way in the industry to present marketing copy. I take a straightforward approach, clearly identifying the headlines, subheads, callouts, sidebars, body copy, and suggestions for visuals. If I have a layout idea or visual concept I can't describe well with words, I attach a rough drawing.

There are numerous ways to present draft copy to your client. Sample 18 shows the format I employ, using a mock print ad as an example.

Sample 18
SUBMITTING AN ASSIGNMENT

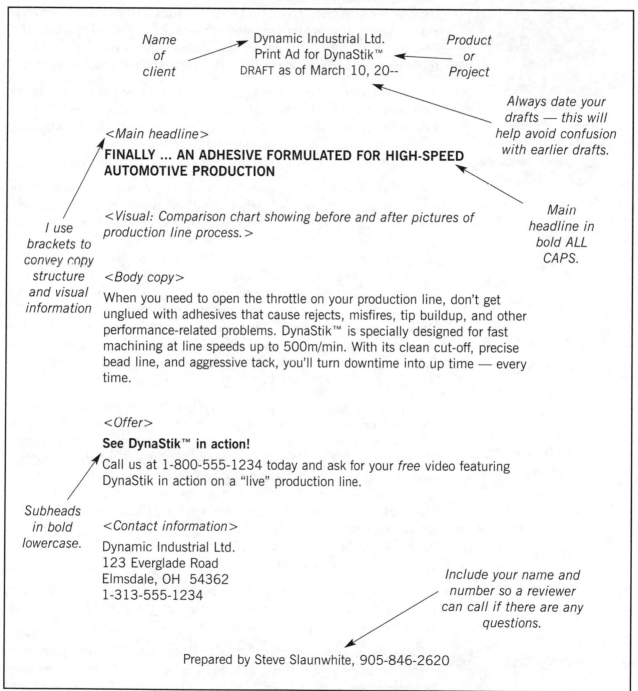

Name of client →

Dynamic Industrial Ltd.
Print Ad for DynaStik™
DRAFT as of March 10, 20--

← Product or Project

Always date your drafts — this will help avoid confusion with earlier drafts.

<Main headline>

FINALLY ... AN ADHESIVE FORMULATED FOR HIGH-SPEED AUTOMOTIVE PRODUCTION

Main headline in bold ALL CAPS.

I use brackets to convey copy structure and visual information

<Visual: Comparison chart showing before and after pictures of production line process.>

<Body copy>

When you need to open the throttle on your production line, don't get unglued with adhesives that cause rejects, misfires, tip buildup, and other performance-related problems. DynaStik™ is specially designed for fast machining at line speeds up to 500m/min. With its clean cut-off, precise bead line, and aggressive tack, you'll turn downtime into up time — every time.

<Offer>

See DynaStik™ in action!

Call us at 1-800-555-1234 today and ask for your *free* video featuring DynaStik in action on a "live" production line.

Subheads in bold lowercase.

<Contact information>

Dynamic Industrial Ltd.
123 Everglade Road
Elmsdale, OH 54362
1-313-555-1234

Include your name and number so a reviewer can call if there are any questions.

Prepared by Steve Slaunwhite, 905-846-2620

Try not to take negative feedback personally. It rarely is personal.

Handling Requests for Revisions

As you become more experienced and develop a savvy for marketing copy, you will receive fewer and fewer requests from clients for revisions. But no copywriter can produce a client-approved draft on the first attempt, every time. It just isn't possible. So you will certainly receive requests from clients for revisions and changes. It's normal.

Unless you've taken the project in a completely different direction than the client expected, most requests for revisions will be minor. They may include corrections in content, the deletion of extraneous information, or clarifications and corrections in facts and data. You'll find these changes quick and easy to make.

But there will be occasions when a client will want you to make a more substantial revision. This could mean reworking one or two sections or, on rare occasions, rewriting the entire piece. For some copywriters, feedback like this is disheartening. When someone requests a complete rewrite, it's easy to doubt your abilities. The most unpleasant feedback I have ever received was from a client a few years ago. A member of the approval committee, someone I had never met or even spoken to, sent my copy back with a giant "X" through each of the pages. I was devastated. It was only weeks later that I found out the feedback was really the result of some political infighting between him and the advertising manager. My copy was fine. I was just being used as cannon fodder.

You'll find some useful ideas on how to handle the challenges of client feedback in Chapter 11. Look under "HELP! My client hates my copy."

When requests for revisions are major, always ask your client for specifics before your proceed with the rewrite. Never attempt to revise copy by relying on vague or unclear comments. Don't accept, "I don't like this section. Please rewrite," without further explanation. You need specifics. To get specifics, you may well have to go over your copy line by line, section by section with your client. Think about it. How many different ways are there to rewrite a sales letter? Dozens? Hundreds? Thousands? So how can you possibly proceed with a rewrite without knowing exactly which sections of your copy need attention, and why?

Most clients will be more than happy to take the time to explain their feedback in detail so you can understand it. After all, they want the best possible copy in the end. And so do you.

You will, however, come across clients who, despite your best efforts, cannot give you the detailed feedback you need. Some may be defensive, even arrogant when you ask them to clarify their comments. Others may simply have difficulty explaining why a particular section doesn't work for them. It's not uncommon to hear a client say, "There's something wrong with this last panel. I just don't know what it is. It doesn't sound right." In these cases, you'll have to help your client by asking specific questions to cull the details.

Always remember that requests for revisions are normal. Try not to sound defensive when discussing such requests with your clients. Simply complete the revision to the best of your ability and send the copy back in. If you feel your client's request is such that it will adversely affect the impact and quality of the piece, you have a duty to point this out. Try to back up your position with facts and provide a good argument. But in the end, it's the client who has the final say. After all, it's the client's copy.

Scheduling Your Time

When you are self-employed with no employees but yourself, your time is your number-one resource. I have found that the best way to manage my time is to schedule it. This sounds easy, but I've actually had to acquire a lot of discipline to do this effectively. I have an inner rebel who doesn't want his time scheduled. He wants the freedom to be lazy and impulsive, to never wear a watch and never be ruled by it. I let him out after work hours. During work hours, I schedule and watch the clock.

In running my own solo business, I have discovered that the loss of just one hour has a high price. A lost hour means I fall behind. A deadline becomes more difficult and stressful to meet. I may have to work that extra hour on the weekend, or another time that otherwise could be spent on leisure activities or with my family. The trouble is, losing an hour is so easy to do. As Harold L. Taylor points out, "We waste minutes shuffling papers, searching for items, forgetting things, interrupting ourselves and others … the list of minutes we waste is almost endless. And minutes do add up to hours." Try not to lose too many.

I have found the best way to effectively schedule my time is hourly and daily. Each morning, I open the scheduling section of my contact management software on my computer and schedule the first two or three hours of my day. I also take a look at my "to do" list for the day, which the software conveniently displays next to my scheduling calendar. Then I proceed with my first hour's work. After that hour is finished, I may take a short break for two or three

In his book *Personal Organization*, Harold L. Taylor points out, "You have 86,400 seconds deposited in your time bank each morning." Use it wisely, and you'll earn a good income as measured against the hours you invest in your business. Fritter it away by being sluggish, unproductive, and focusing too much on unimportant activities, and your business will be filled with long hours and short pay.

minutes, get up and stretch, get a coffee, and start into the next hour. I do this hour-by-hour routine throughout the day.

Of course, a copywriter's day can change from hour to hour, so I freely update my schedule if a new project comes in, or if my priorities get jostled.

Years ago, I followed a similar process using a traditional appointment book or organizer. If you don't want to invest in scheduling software, you can do the same. In fact, many professionals, even those who are computer savvy, still prefer to schedule their work and their time with pen and paper. There are lots of organizers, schedulers, and time-management products on the market — you'll find a selection in your local business supply store. But the best I have ever come across is marketed by Taylor Time Systems, Inc., and is not available in stores. Check out their website at <www.TaylorOnTime.com> for more information.

If you do decide to use a paper-based system, here's a trick I learned that can save you lots of confusion and mess. When scheduling and writing notes in your organizer, use a pencil, not a pen. Pencils are softer, look neater, are less messy, and can be erased (which is handy because a copywriter's schedule frequently changes). Pens are permanent and leave ink on your hands.

Tips for Improving Your Productivity

Being productive is a great way to improve your income in two ways. First, you can more often meet client demands. Second, you'll complete more billable work in less time. If it takes you four hours to complete a $500 sales letter, for example, and you find ways to improve your productivity so you can complete the same letter in three hours, you've just given yourself a $40 per hour raise!

Here are some productivity tips I have found that have really helped.

Keep regular hours

I recently watched a documentary on ABBA, perhaps the most successful pop group in history (next to the Beatles). During the show, the interviewer asked one half of the writing team, Benny Anderssen, how they managed to write such a long string of highly successful songs — songs that have sold tens of millions of records. His reply? To paraphrase, he said, "I showed up to work each day. I kept a workperson's hours."

There is a fallacy among some writers that great creative work comes from sudden moments of inspiration when the "muse" strikes. The trouble with this is that the muse isn't always around when you need her. And you still have to get the work done. The fact is, most successful creative professionals I know keep regular hours plying their craft each day.

Start at the same time each day. Because I'm more productive in the morning, I start at seven. Your productive time may be later in the day. Find a starting time most productive for you and stick with it.

Write during your power hours

You'll write and complete client tasks more productively if you do so during your peak hours. For most people, this is the mornings. However, you might also be an afternoon/evening person. I once read that prolific Canadian writer Ann Douglas writes in the evenings because that's when her house is quieter (she has a number of kids, and writes about parenting).

When working on client projects, you'll be doing a lot of writing and thinking. Do these during the part of the day when you are most refreshed. For me, this is the morning. Sometimes early morning. In fact, when I have to put in a long day, I start *earlier*; I don't work later. Schedule your other business tasks — such as returning calls, attending meetings, bookkeeping, and running errands — for when your energy level ebbs.

Stay seated

Years ago, while still in high school, I attended a writer's workshop facilitated by a successful novelist. When asked what, in his opinion, is the most important advice he could give a fledgling writer, he said, "Stay seated. Don't get up until you've reached your writing goal for the day." I agree with this advice.

When you're working solo, it's easy to procrastinate. You'll find yourself having moments of laziness. You'll get up to go to the kitchen to drink a glass of water, and before you know it you're clicking on the television "just to get a few moments of the news." Soon a half hour, or even an hour has passed.

In the classic book, *On Writing Well*, author William Zinsser says, "Writing is a craft, not an art ... the man who runs away from his craft because he lacks inspiration is fooling himself. He is also going broke."

Since I block out my work schedule in one-hour increments, staying seated — and therefore productive — is easier for me. Once I commit to doing a particular task for one hour, from 9:00 a.m. to 10:00 a.m., for example, I sit there and don't move until 10:00 a.m. At ten, I can take a break, walk around, and plan my next hour.

I'm not the most disciplined person in the world. Far from it. But I can sit and work on a project for just one hour. And so can you.

Separate work from home

If you work from home, you have a built-in distraction. The rest of your house! The comfy living room. The television. The fridge. Your kids. To stay productive, you must find ways to separate your work space from your home space. Working at the kitchen table, for example, with kids playing in the next room can be counter-productive. Try, if you can, to create a work area apart from the rest of your home. This could be a room in the basement with a door you can close. Or a bedroom converted to an office space. Use this room only as an office, and for nothing else. For suggestions on work space planning, see Chapter 3.

Invest in productivity-boosting ideas

If you come across tools, software, procedures, or methodologies you suspect might improve your productivity, invest in them.

Always be looking for things and ideas that can help you work faster and with less stress. I recently came across the idea of a numerical filing system, and put it into practice. In the past, like most people, I filed alphabetically. But I found it a chore to find files. Did I file it under "S" for The Simons Group, or under "T" for The? Then there was the issue of duplicate files, and being unable to find information because it was contained in a file folder I had forgotten even existed.

By filing numerically, creating and finding a file is easy. When I need to create a new file, I simply use the next available number. To find a file, I keep an alpha-numerical listing as a hardcopy on top of my filing cabinet. I also maintain a computer file. When I need to find the file containing my banking records, for example, I simply push the search button, type "banking" and it finds the file and corresponding file number. Then I go to my filing cabinet and get it. Numerical filing saves me hours. And I never misplace a file.

My office has only office furniture in it. It's used only for business purposes. It even has a separate phone line. When I walk into my "office" and close the door, I'm at work.

Minimize time spent on non-billable tasks

Unfortunately, you will not be paid for every hour you work. You'll be involved in a number of non-billable tasks. These are the hours you spend filing, bookkeeping, ordering supplies, creating marketing materials, making sales calls — all the tasks that need doing, but will not be billed directly to a client.

Obviously, the more time you spend working on paying client assignments, and the less time you spend managing other aspects of your business, the more income you'll earn. So you need to continually find ways to minimize your time spent on non-billable activities.

One way is to invest in software and systems that help improve your productivity. I have accounting software designed for small businesses, so that all I have to do is diligently input my sales, expenditures, and checks. The software does the rest; it keeps records and creates all the financial reports I need. The only problem is, I have to keep the records updated. If I fall behind, I'm faced with a mountain of receipts to input. And that's no fun.

You can also hire someone else to do some non-billable tasks for you. For example, I often tape record interviews when I write case studies and annual reports. An interview can take anywhere from a few minutes to an hour or more. To transcribe these would take me even more hours. But I have found a local source — a women who offers business support services from her home office — who can do it for me in less time.

"But you have to pay her," you might say. "How does that save you money?" I don't pass this expense on to my clients. But the hours her transcribing services save me are hours I can spend on billable tasks. Since my hourly rate to clients is higher than hers, the money I invest in her services pays off.

You might find similar outside sources to handle such things as stuffing envelopes for a mailing, sending out invoices and managing receivables, and running errands to the bank or post office. Copywriter Bob Bly often boasts, "I haven't been to the post office in ten years." He has someone else do this time-consuming chore for him.

Stay organized

Sometimes, when I get very busy, I let some things slip — like filing, bookkeeping, and other necessary components to good organization.

You can learn how to use accounting programs and other software through courses offered at local public schools, colleges, and universities.

And I pay the price. I have found it takes far less time to stay organized than it does to get organized. There is nothing more miserable than spending a Saturday morning filing or going through the stack in your in tray, because you've let these tasks slip for a few days. Or weeks. (Trust me, I know exactly how this feels!)

Good organization is not my strength. I have to work at it. But staying organized does make me feel more in control. There are plenty of books and resources available that will teach you to stay organized and efficient. I have found that investing just 15 minutes each day in keeping my work area and business organized — paying bills, filing, returning calls — actually saves me time in the long run. I sleep better, knowing an important detail hasn't fallen through the cracks because of disorganization.

Watch the Money

There is a saying among the self-employed that "Cash is King." Your ability to manage your cash flow and maintain the optimum balance in your bank account will be due to your diligence in watching the money. If you don't watch closely, money has an amazing tendency to trickle away. There's nothing more miserable than a plummeting cash account with no client checks in sight for two or three months.

Here are the methods I follow in managing the cash flow of my copywriting business.

Sending invoices

You should have a clear, specific policy for when you send invoices to clients. Are you going to send your invoice immediately after you complete and submit your draft? After your first revision? Once the piece is produced? What if a project gets held up by the client midway through? What if the project gets canceled, and you have already completed some of the work?

There should be no confusion between you and your client about invoicing. With every assignment, I get a signed quotation/agreement from the client (see Sample 10 in Chapter 7). It describes, in detail, how and when I invoice.

Invoicing

An invoice is sent one week after your receipt of the initial draft, payable net 30 days. Should you cancel or place this project on hold for any reason, you will be invoiced for all work completed to date.

There are plenty of books on managing money for your home-based business. One book I recommend for this is *Financial Management 101: Get a Grip on Your Business Numbers*, by Angie Mohr (Self-Counsel Press).

I suggest you include your invoicing policy up front in your contract or agreement.

In my experience, sending a client invoice one week after completing and submitting the draft copy is appropriate. This gives the client more than enough time to read and absorb the copy and request revisions. In my agreement with clients, revisions are completed at no charge for up to 60 days. So even if they receive and pay my invoice, they can still get the copy revised by me if necessary.

I print out my invoice on my own letterhead. I simply mark INVOICE on the top, and include the following information:

- Client's name

- Client's purchase order number

- Docket number (important when the invoice is to a graphic design firm or advertising agency)

- Name of the person who authorized the job

- Brief description of the assignment

- Quoted fee (If the amount is above the quoted fee, explain, in detail, the reason.)

- Taxes applied

- Advance paid by the client before you began the job, if any

- Total owed by the client (fee plus taxes less advance)

- Your terms (net 30 days, or payable upon receipt)

- Listing of any expenses you paid that will be passed on to the client (You must also submit original receipts, but retain photocopies in case the originals are lost.)

Sample 19 is an example of an invoice.

More clients these days are requesting that invoices be sent by e-mail. This is easy to do. Simply prepare the invoice as you would normally then, instead of printing it, create a PDF (Portable Document Format). The next step is to attach it, as a file attachment, in an e-mail to your client. In seconds, you're done.

INVOICE

DATE: June 30, 20--

INVOICE NO: 1525

To:

DynaComm Communications
999 Vanderhoof Avenue
Toronto, ON M4G 4C9

Purchase Order: 98765
Docket Number: DYA-4567
Authorization: John Anderson
GST# 894529841

QUANTITY	DESCRIPTION	UNIT PRICE	AMOUNT
1	Copywriting: Full-page print advertisement for DynaStik	875.00	$875.00

SUBTOTAL	$875.00
GST 7%	61.25
TOTAL DUE	$936.25

Payable upon receipt.
Kindly make your check payable to: SLAUNWHITE COMMUNICATIONS

THANKS FOR YOUR BUSINESS!

Getting paid

Clients will typically pay your invoice 45 to 90 days after you send it. But, unfortunately, some will need a little prodding. In fact, I know one small ad agency that will not pay an invoice until they receive reminder letters. For them to pay your legitimate invoice, you actually have to beg! Fortunately, this type of client is rare.

I send a friendly reminder letter (see Sample 20) after my invoice has aged 45 days and every two weeks after that until my invoice is paid. I also call to ask for the payment status of my invoice.

Many self-employed professionals don't like tracking invoices and asking for payment. To them, I suspect, it brings to mind Mafioso money collectors from the movies. But asking for prompt payment on legitimate invoices is normal business practice. In fact, your clients probably do the same thing. And it's easy. All you do is call and say, "I'd like to follow up on my invoice number …"

If you ever have difficulty getting a client to pay your invoice, or if you suspect he or she is stalling or does not intend to pay, you have to get more assertive in your approach. I tackle this problem in Chapter 11. See, "HELP! A client won't pay my invoice!"

Keeping good books

When it comes to keeping records of the financial aspects of your business, don't take the shoebox approach. Never allow receipts to pile up in a drawer or let your bank account go unbalanced for months. Be a diligent, organized, and accurate bookkeeper. If you can't, find a local bookkeeping service to do it for you.

There are plenty of accounting software products on the market that can help. I use *QuickBooks*, which I find very easy to use. At the end of a month, quarter, or year, I can print off all my business's financial reports with a few clicks of the mouse. I can also see my income statement partway through the month to see how I'm doing.

There are many other small-business accounting software products on the market that are, perhaps, just as good as the one I use. *MYOB* and *Simply Accounting* are two very popular products.

"Some organizations take a disgracefully long time to settle invoices, even if they relate to work which has increased both their customers' and their own profits," says Diana Wimbs in her book *Freelance Copywriting*. "This reluctance to pay is insidious and could affect you whether you are writing directly for the organization concerned or one of its' agencies."

Sample 20
FRIENDLY REMINDER LETTER

August 16, 20--

ChapMor Components Inc.
500 Wyecroft Road
Syracuse, NY 45361

Just a friendly reminder ...

ATT: Rick Douglas

Thanks for asking me to contribute to the production of your brochure promoting ChapMor Industrial Widgets. I enjoyed working with you and your team.

For your information, the invoice I sent for this project has just aged 45 days and is now past due. Here are the details:

    Authorization: Rick Douglas
    Purchase Order: 00263
    Invoice number: 1528
    Invoice date: June 30, 20--
    Amount due: $1,070.00

Could you please send payment at your earliest convenience? If you have any questions or concerns, feel free to call me anytime.

Sincerely,

Steve Slaunwhite

Steve Slaunwhite

P.S. Of course, if you have already sent payment, please disregard this notice.

Some Final Advice

A few years ago, a successful self-employed professional told me, "Steve, there are three things you have to do well to succeed on your own. One, get the business. Two, do the business. And three, run the business." At the time, I didn't fully appreciate what he was telling me. In fact, I wasn't entirely sure I believed him. But I sure do now!

During my first year in business, I felt like I was pouring wine into a stack of wine glasses; each one filling and overflowing into the next. For the first few months I poured most of my energy into finding clients and getting assignments; virtually ignoring all other aspects of my business. Then, once I had completed a few client projects, I realized I had better learn to "do the business" — that is, write copy — a lot better. So I read and studied and practiced. Then tax time came, and I realized, to my surprise, I wasn't "running the business" all too well. So I spent two miserable weeks trying to make sense of the bundles of invoices and receipts crammed into the second drawer of my desk.

To succeed as a self-employed copywriter, you have to learn to do many things — find clients, complete orders, manage your time, handle money — very well. So, if you're just starting out in this business, you're going to make some mistakes (I sure did). You may find it tough, at times, to get business. You might run out of money. You may have to face an angry client who doesn't like your work or won't pay your invoice. Deadline stress and cash flow worries might get you down. You might even doubt if being self-employed is worth the headaches. Don't worry. Every self-employed professional I know has had this same feeling.

Guess what? You're going to face challenges in your copywriting business. Many challenges. The first year is probably going to be the toughest (however, many freelancers say their first year was also the most rewarding). Problems come with the territory. Fortunately, there are solutions, many of which you'll find in the next chapter.

You're also going to have many good times. There is nothing more satisfying than receiving copies of the recently printed brochure or direct-mail piece you wrote, and seeing a sticky note from your client saying, "Great job. We'll definitely use your services again!" It feels almost as good as receiving the check a few weeks later!

The trick to staying sane and happy in this business is balance. Keep your focus equally on getting the business, doing the business, and running the business. Be aware of periods when you let one or two of these areas slide, because then you're on a certain road to trouble. Maintain balance, and you'll reach your business goals a lot sooner.

11
Troubleshooting Guide

Despite your best laid plans, you are bound to experience unexpected turbulence in your copywriting business. Problems will pop up out of nowhere. Issues you never anticipated will suddenly throw you a curve. These will cause stress and worry that will rob you of your most precious commodity: Your time.

In this chapter, I list some of the more common problems faced by self-employed copywriters, then detail what I and other copywriters do to solve them.

The following list does not cover every contingency. Far from it. But most freelance copywriters would agree that these represent a good 80 percent of the bumps and tumbles you'll likely experience during your freelance career.

Proven Solutions to Common Problems

"HELP! My client complains my quote is too high!"

No doubt, despite following the advice on quoting projects in Chapter 7, a prospective client will call and say, "Ouch! Your quote is a little more than I expected!" You'll find this happens with new clients more than with current clients. After all, your current clients are familiar with your fee range and have direct experience with the value of your work. However, when someone does complain about your quoted fee, don't panic. And never, ever immediately cave to a lower price.

Check to see if both you and the client fully understand the scope of the project. For example, if the project is writing a promotional newsletter, confirm with the client that the job involves developing article ideas, research, interviewing contacts, writing, and handling rewrites. If your client says, "No, I'll provide you with all the research, interview transcripts, and article ideas you need. I just want you to write the copy," then the misunderstanding lies with you. Simply apologize and offer to requote based on your new understanding of the scope of the project. (Keep in mind, in this particular example, you will likely have to do some research and interviewing.)

But what if you understood the project perfectly and your prospect still demands a lower price? In this case, the problem may lie with your client — not you. He or she may not understand or fully appreciate the work involved. This is especially true of junior buyers of creative services who may never have hired a copywriter before. You'll have to explain the process — the time required to set up telephone interviews, research, develop topics, write, rewrite, and coordinate your efforts with the art director or design firm.

If your client still insists on paying less, there are few options left. You can meet the price and complete the assignment. You can negotiate a compromise and meet in the middle. Or you can turn down the project, explaining that your professional fees are set and that another copywriter may be more suited to the client's needs and budget. (You might even recommend another copywriter.)

I would like to say I have always stayed firm on my quoted price and proudly never compromised, but this isn't true. The fact is, I have used all three of the above options when faced with a price objection. I have met a client's desired fee. I have renegotiated. And I have walked away. I can report to you that meeting a client's lower price — especially when it is substantially lower — is a mistake. I'll never do it again, no matter how hungry I get. Once a client realizes he or she can get your services at cut rate, the client will expect the same on future projects. And, trust me, it doesn't matter how many times you tell your client the lower fee is "applied to that one project only."

It's much better to renegotiate. After all, a client may have legitimate reasons for wanting a lower price. If your quote for a direct-mail package is $3,500 and your client has an approved budget of only $3,100, is there room to negotiate? Of course there is. If I really want to work with a particular client and there is a price objection, I'll say, "John, I think we can work together very successfully on this project. Let's work out a price we can both live with and get started."

A final word about renegotiating your price. Beware of hard luck stories from ad agencies and design firms. You'll hear things like, "We already paid another writer, and the copy she wrote was unacceptable. So we don't have much money left to pay you to fix it." Or, "We didn't quote our client for copywriting so we don't have it in the budget. Can you give us a break on your fees?" In these cases, the agency or design firm is asking for a favor. They are asking you to bail them out (by sacrificing a portion of your fees to sustain their margins). If you sincerely want to help them, that's fine. But remember: It's their problem, not yours. You have every right to insist on your normal, professional fees.

"HELP! I have more work than I can handle!"

You've worked hard to promote your services and deliver great work to your clients. Your business and reputation are growing. But now work is flooding in, and you have more than you can handle. What do you do?

This isn't an easy situation. You either have to work longer hours, work faster, or turn down work.

When I get overloaded with assignments — a frequent situation these days — I'll work longer hours. I have found a fairly painless way to do this by getting up an hour early. I usually start at 7:00 a.m. because, by nature, I'm a morning person. By getting out of bed an hour early, I can start at 6:00 a.m. Over a two-week period, this adds up to another ten hours. More than an extra full day!

If I am really busy, I will also work weekend mornings for two or three hours, but I prefer not to. On weekends, I need to recharge my batteries and spend time with my family.

Another approach is to work faster. This doesn't mean typing faster or working in a stressed-out, mad flurry, but by having a more dedicated focus on the writing tasks at hand, I'm able to complete them sooner. When I'm busy, I will put all extraneous business activities on the back burner. I won't read the mail or any business magazines that come in. I'll leave bookkeeping, filing, and other office tasks until the busy period is over, and I'll put long-term projects on hold.

You may reach a point when working faster and longer is no longer practical. The flood of work you have been receiving may not be temporary, but a new reality for your business. Getting up early, working faster, and putting off business tasks for weeks or months will only lead to disaster. In this case, you may have to turn down work.

You'll find saying "no" tough, because you've worked hard to attract clients and now you're turning them away! I received a call yesterday from a potential client and had to say I was booked solid with work until the end of next month. She was shocked. (Fortunately, I was able to refer another copywriter who reportedly is working out great.)

If you must turn down work, start with potential clients only. Avoid, if you can, turning down work from a current client. After all, with potential clients you have nothing to lose because you have never worked with them before. They may even be impressed that you're so busy, and call again on a future project. But with current clients, you've invested in the relationship and there is long-term repeat business at stake. When you turn them down, you let them down. They'll have to call someone else, another copywriter who fills your shoes at your now former account. Permanently.

Another option I have never personally explored is hiring an assistant or outsourcing certain business tasks to outside services. But, as I become increasingly busy, I am considering this approach. I hate filing, bookkeeping, depositing checks, and managing my various marketing efforts. I prefer to deal with clients, think, create, and write. So I may soon be on the lookout for an assistant or an office service to help with auxiliary business tasks.

"HELP! My client has given me an impossible deadline!"

What do you do when your best client calls with a great project — and a daunting deadline? You don't want to turn down the project and open the doors to another copywriter. At the same time, the deadline may be impossible to accommodate. Or you may be able to meet the deadline, but only with a sacrifice in quality. Quite a dilemma.

I have found that the best approach when hit with a deadline I cannot accommodate is to negotiate. Most deadlines are arbitrarily set. Clients understandably want to get completed work in from outside vendors earlier rather than later. It avoids stress. But if the deadline is too tight, you can often request and get a more realistic deadline. For example, if a client calls and asks if I can have copy completed by this Friday, I say something like, "Friday is tough, perhaps impossible. But what would happen if I got the copy to you the following Tuesday at 9:00 a.m.?" In most cases the client will say "Sure, Tuesday's fine." I have found that 80 percent of tight deadlines set by clients can be negotiated using this friendly, non-confrontational approach.

In a very few cases, the stringent deadline the client has set is very real. There may be a trade show date to meet or a print advertising deadline that cannot be missed. In these cases, you have few choices. You can either accept the deadline and do the best job you can, or turn your client down.

What do I do? If my client is really in a jam, I usually accept the deadline, with the understanding that working under this type of pressure is not my normal business practice. If the deadline is truly impossible for me to meet, regardless of how late I work, I have no choice. I turn the assignment down.

"HELP! I don't have any assignments!"

If you have run out of work, and the phone isn't ringing, don't panic. This is an ebb and flow business, and busy/slow cycles are normal. But a slow period, however temporary, doesn't mean you can rest on your laurels. There's plenty to do.

A slow period can also be a time to relax and recharge — especially if you've just come off a very busy stretch. But don't relax too much. Remember that when times are slow, you're not invoicing as much. And you're going to feel the effects of this, in terms of cash flow, two or three months down the road.

If you have created a lead-generating machine, as described in chapter 5, then pull the lever! Generate the leads you need to develop new business. This approach works much better, however, when you can anticipate a slow period. After all, it takes time (perhaps months) for a cluster of leads to develop into clients and orders.

Let's say you have plenty of client work to keep you busy for the next two months. Great. But don't wait two months to pull the lever on your lead-generating machine. Pull it now! Get some leads so that when the time comes, those leads will have developed into some business.

Slow times can be a blessing in disguise. They give you time to tweak your marketing efforts: do some self-promotion, write an article for a marketing magazine, create your website, learn something new. During my last slow period, I learned all about business-to-business e-mail marketing. This knowledge has paid off tremendously.

Some freelancers say that when business is slow, you should call your list of clients to let them know you're available. I disagree. It places you in a hungry, weak position and may, in fact, have the opposite effect. Clients want to do business with copywriters who are successful — not those who seem to be desperately scrambling for business. If you've written good copy and provided good services, your past clients will call when an assignment comes up. They haven't forgotten you.

"HELP! A client won't pay my invoice!"

There is nothing more frustrating than spending valuable time chasing a client for payment of a long-overdue invoice. Copywriter Alan Sharpe lists the top two things he likes *least* about the copywriting business: "Not being paid on time," and "Having to send clients a first, second, third, and fourth late notice for unpaid invoices."

Fortunately, it's not as common as you might expect. Perhaps I'm lucky in that most of my clients pay my invoices promptly — within 60 days. Still, a couple of times each year, I'll have to pursue payment for an invoice that is aging. ("Aging" refers to the time an invoice is outstanding, usually in increments of 30 days.)

The best approach to managing outstanding invoices and reducing stress is to create a regimen of phone calls and letters. I send out a polite "reminder" letter after an invoice has aged 45 days.

At 60 days, the two-month mark, I send another reminder letter *and* I make a phone call. I ask for the person in charge of accounts payable, and say, "Hi, this is Steve Slaunwhite calling. I'm calling to follow up on my invoice dated ..." Usually, he or she will tell me that payment is forthcoming and approximately when a check will "be cut."

If payment isn't received by the 75-day point, I send another letter — a little sterner this time. I continue to send letters and make calls until the invoice is paid.

If an invoice passes the 90-day point, that's a sign of trouble. This is especially true if your client is not giving you a clear explanation of why your invoice isn't being paid, or, worse, is not returning your calls. You'll have to keep calling and sending letters, letting your client know you will not give up and you expect your invoice to be paid.

Generally, the longer an invoice is outstanding, the less likely it will be paid. So you'll have to be relentless after the 90-day point. Don't be afraid to inform your client that, if payment is not received soon, you'll have to submit your invoice to a lawyer, a collections agency, or court. If they still don't pay, follow through on your threat.

You can hedge many potential payment problems by being proactive. Make sure you get a signed authorization for every job you do. If you doubt a client's ability to pay, or if the client is a small business or agency, ask for an advance payment *before* you start work (20 percent to 50 percent is normal). If the client balks at paying your advance, your suspicions are confirmed.

Working with larger companies can also protect you from payment hassles. If your client is a large, well-established ad agency or Fortune 500 corporation, the chance of your legitimate invoice being paid is very high.

"HELP! My client hates my copy!"

I'm lucky. Much of the work I submit to clients is accepted with no requests for revisions. Of the requests for revisions I do receive,

When following up on your invoice, ask for the person in charge of "accounts payable." This is the person who can most quickly determine if and when payment will be sent.

Some self-employed friends claim they get embarrassed by calling a client and asking for payment on an invoice. Nonsense. You have every right as a businessperson to rigorously track and follow up outstanding invoices. When your invoice is overdue, never be afraid to call your client to ask when payment can be expected.

most are very minor. But this track record doesn't mean I'm immune to negative feedback.

Writing is often judged subjectively. I once wrote a website that six members of the management team loved — and one member hated. It's hard not to take it personally. But it rarely is personal.

Here are some guidelines I follow when I receive less-than-complimentary feedback from clients.

Don't be defensive

If you receive negative comments on your copy, even if the client seems upset and angry, stay professional. Don't adopt a defensive tone or posture. You want feedback, not combat. Listen carefully, and try to determine what went wrong. With a deadline approaching, your client may very well be nervous that the copy cannot be fixed. Clients may want to blow off steam. Unless it becomes personally abusive, let them.

Explain your approach

Sometimes you will make a creative decision that the client doesn't immediately understand. A client once told me he hated the word "Free," thought it was a tired cliché, and didn't want it used in his direct mail. Once I explained the word "Free" is timeless, proven effective, and worked well with the other elements of his package, he agreed to keep it in.

Just a few weeks ago, an ad agency director phoned me in a panic complaining that my copy was too long and had too many technical buzzwords. But when I told him the piece was targeted at IT and systems managers, and explained the importance of using their vernacular, he understood. When he presented the copy to his client, it was quickly approved.

Ask for specifics

Never accept vague feedback like, "Paragraph three just doesn't grab me," or "I don't like the fourth panel." Nail down specifics. Ask your client the following questions:

- "Have I included all the key messages?"
- "Are they presented in the best order, from most important to least important?"

- "Is the content accurate?"

- "Are the benefits fully explained?"

- "Are there passages that seem unclear or confusing?"

- "Is there extraneous information that should be deleted?"

- "Is the writing style too formal? Too casual? Too technical? Not technical enough?"

By asking specific questions, you have a good chance of getting specific answers. You also demonstrate to the client your professionalism, thoroughness, and willingness to dig deep to revise the copy to his or her satisfaction.

A client may say something like: "I can't describe what I want. But I'll know it when I read it." If a client cannot, or will not, give you specific feedback, explain that you can't work in the dark. If he or she will not work with you to identify and clarify problem areas, tell the client it's impossible to proceed with the rewrite (because it *is* impossible).

Fortunately, most clients will be helpful during the revision process. After all, they want great copy just as much as you do.

Don't be afraid to go through your copy section by section, line by line if necessary, to flush out the problem areas. Always strive to uncover specifics. Never attempt to guess your way through a rewrite.

Confirm

Once you've gone through your copy and identified and clarified areas that require revision, confirm these details with your client. Some copywriters will actually put these details in writing, but, in my experience, this time-consuming step is unnecessary. I simply verbally summarize with the client what needs to be accomplished. If he or she agrees with my understanding, I proceed with the revision.

Set a deadline

Never say, "I'll turn this revision around in a couple of days." Always confirm exactly when you'll complete and submit the new, revised draft. In my office, I treat each revision as if it's a new project. I assign a deadline, and confirm this deadline with my client.

Complete the revision exactly as directed

Being a creative person, you'll be tempted to add new angles and other ideas to the copy you've already written. But the time for this stage of copy development has passed. You and your client have agreed to a specific set of revisions. Do these well, and nothing else.

Remember, your first submitted draft has likely triggered a series of events. Illustrations and other artwork may already be planned and ordered. The designer may be working on a layout scheme based on your copy. Any ideas you submit now may very well tip the apple cart.

If you do find yourself overwhelmed with a new idea for the copy, call your client or send an e-mail. Don't make changes to the existing copy until you've received approval to go ahead and incorporate your new idea.

"HELP! I can't stay motivated!"

A temporary inability to concentrate and stay motivated is likely a sign of stress or fatigue. As a self-employed copywriter, you'll spend hours each day thinking and writing. It's hard work. Not hard *physical* work, by any means, but hard mental work. It requires focus. However, when you're overloaded with assignments, client demands, and the daily pressures of running your own business, you'll need to recharge your batteries every once in a while.

Here are some things I do to relieve stress and fatigue:

- *Take a walk.* I live near a lake with a walking path. Sometimes a 15-minute stroll around the lake is all I need to regenerate.

- *Take a break.* Once every hour or so I'll get up and stretch. You'll be surprised how effective a five-minute break can be. But avoid taking longer breaks. Once you've relaxed for more than a hour, it's difficult to get back to the grind.

- *Switch gears.* If you have multiple projects on the go, you have an advantage. When you get tired of one project, you can simply switch to another.

- *Take a day off.* One of the great things about being self-employed is that you can plan a day off any time. So plan one! If you're tired and feel overworked, a day off in the sunshine, or shopping, or just relaxing around the house can do wonders. Just the act of planning a day off can give you a lift.

- *Treat yourself.* Sometimes I'll take myself out for a coffee and tea biscuit at a local café. It's a nice treat that takes only a half hour or so out of my day.

- *Plan a vacation.* Having something to look forward to can be a great stress reliever. I feel relaxed just by flipping through travel brochures!

- *Exercise.* Exercise is a proven stress management tool. You might join a gym, walk, jog, or ride your bike after work. In your copywriting business, you'll spend hours sitting, so exercise is a nice — and recommended — change of pace.

If you find that your lack of motivation just won't let up, this could be a sign of other problems. You may need a longer break from your business, a sabbatical, if you can afford it. See your doctor if it doesn't let up.

"HELP! I have to back out of an assignment!"

It's bound to happen. In your eagerness to find clients and ply your copywriting craft, you'll take on a project you later regret. This may be because you're overloaded with other assignments, or the project you've taken on is not what you expected. This can place you in a very uncomfortable position. You can either complete the job as best you can, or drop out of the assignment, which creates a negative impression of you with your client.

Quitting an assignment in mid-stream because you find it morally objectionable is a little easier than dropping out just because you're busy. When you back out because you've taken on more projects than you can handle, the client feels blown off and unimportant. "Why me and not some other client?" he or she thinks.

If you have quoted and accepted an assignment, I suggest you do your best to follow through and complete it. This creates far fewer problems. If you must drop out, be professional. Contact the client by phone and explain that you must drop out. No need to go into unnecessary details. Simply apologize for the inconvenience and, if you can, recommend another copywriter.

I suggest you cultivate a network of other copywriters in your area whom you can refer. I would never suggest you give away your best client to a competing copywriter, but if you're stuck and cannot take on a client project, your client will appreciate your helpfulness.

Recommend only those copywriters you are familiar with and trust. Consider trading portfolio samples to gauge each other's work (they may also refer you). Chat with them on the phone. Trade war stories. I have developed a small network of local copywriters I regularly refer — and they refer me. It's a win-win situation.

"HELP! The client I'm working with is a jerk!"

Ivan Levison, a highly successful freelance copywriter, says, "For me, being self-employed means I have the right to work with only nice people." I agree. The great thing about being self-employed is that, to a large extent, you get to choose your own clients. If you're having frequent personality conflicts with a particular client, you can complete any projects you have on the go and close the account. You won't be doing yourself, or your client, any favors by accepting further assignments.

"But I'm still struggling," you might say. "I can't afford to give up clients just because I don't like them." I completely understand. I've done plenty of business with people I didn't particularly like so I could pay my bills and feed my family. When you're self-employed, it goes with the territory. But when a client is continually unreasonable, verbally abusive, or just plain rubs you the wrong way, you'll be doing yourself an enormous service by letting go.

I recently read an article about a public relations professional who "fired" her client — the CEO of a major corporation — because he called from the airport at four in the morning to ask for a limousine. I'm sure letting that client go gave her ego a lift.

If you have a client you're just not getting along with, or, worse, who has become miserable to work for, say goodbye. You don't have to be dramatic about it. Simply decide not to accept any further assignments from this client and get on with the rest of your business.

"HELP! I can't get all the information I need from my client to complete the job!"

Often, with copywriting assignments, you'll find yourself working with incomplete information. This is especially true of longer, more complex projects such as annual reports, brochures, and websites. You may find that client contacts are not returning your calls or e-mail as quickly as you hoped. Or that key project information you need has not arrived when expected.

It's not uncommon for a client to reply to your query with something like, "Call Rosie in our service department. She'll know." And you call Rosie, only to find she's on holiday.

You may even come across situations in which certain facts are actually in dispute. Ralph in marketing says the widget has a 2 percent return record. Janice in customer service balks with, "Two? More like five!" Who's right? Which fact do you use in your copy?

Here are some guidelines I use when I have to work with incomplete information, or I'm having difficulty getting the information I need to effectively complete an assignment.

- *Be persistent.* If you need information from a client or anyone else in your client's organization, keep calling and e-mailing. Explain, politely, that you need the information to properly complete the project.

- *Be proactive.* Try to find the information yourself. Maybe it's buried in the stack of background information the client gave you. In many cases, I have found exactly the information I needed on a client's website.

- *Never guess.* When you have less than the information you need, there is a tendency to fill in the gaps yourself. Intuition is a great thing and you may even guess right much of the time. But you'll also guess wrong equally as much, thus wasting time. Don't guess. Get the facts.

- *Meet the deadline, no matter what.* Never threaten not to meet a deadline because of missing information. Always submit the best draft you can based on the information at hand. You can leave a section of your draft empty, simply stating: "Information for this section forthcoming from John Smith." Or Ralph or Jill or whomever owes you the information you need.

"HELP! My client wants a teleconference. What the heck is that?"

When I started in this business, teleconferencing was rare. Now there's a teleconference speaker set on every boardroom table in America!

As a freelance copywriter, you're bound to be invited to attend a teleconference meeting to brainstorm ideas, review concepts, or discuss project details. This is especially true if you're dealing with large agencies or corporate clients. These days, corporate managers have tight schedules and often travel extensively. It's difficult, if not impossible, to get everyone in the same room at the same time. So virtual meetings have become the norm.

This is good news for freelance copywriters because, instead of getting dressed up and traveling to meet with clients — which can waste hours of your time — you can attend a meeting in the comfort of your own office. (In your pajamas, if you like!)

Here's how it works:

Typically, the person arranging the teleconference, usually the manager in charge of the project, will e-mail the teleconference details. You'll receive a special dial-in number (usually toll free) and an access code. On the day and time of the teleconference, simply dial the number, punch in the access code, and you're in.

Here are some useful teleconference meeting tips:

- Obviously, you can't see anybody. All you can hear are voices. So when the introductions take place, write down the names on a piece of paper. This will help you keep track of who's saying what during the discussions.

- If you're one of the first few people to "arrive" at the teleconference, it's normal to chit-chat before the other participants call in. But be careful what you say! Avoid negative talk about people who haven't arrived on the call yet. They could be there already, quietly listening to every word you say!

- Teleconferences can sometimes drag on. But stay tuned in. Don't do anything that is distracting, such as surfing the Internet, doodling, or working on other projects. You want to be able to give a good answer when you're called on for an opinion.

- Ask if you can be added to the e-mail list of anyone who is taking notes. And take good notes yourself, too. Don't assume that you will automatically receive a summary of the call. You may not.

"HELP! My client wants me to do more work than I bargained for."

Sometimes a client will ask for, or expect, more work from you than you had originally agreed to do. This can range from a relatively minor request for an additional blurb on a website to an out-and-out misunderstanding as to who was supposed to provide the artwork to go with your copy.

Here's what can happen:

- The client casts you in the role of "project manager," expecting that you will take charge of coordinating design, sourcing lists, and arranging meetings.

- The client wants you to do extensive research, digging up facts that don't currently exist in the background materials he or she sent you.

- The client wants you to work closely with the designer, suggesting layout strategies, ordering revisions, and even presenting concepts.

- The client asks you to provide alternative versions of the copy, so he or she can pick the one he or she likes best.

- The client wants you to submit the copy in HTML (Internet language), or even publish the copy online.

- The client changes the direction of the project, adding more pages or topics to be covered.

- The client innocently asks you, "While you're writing the brochure, can you think of a new slogan for the product, too?"

The best way to avoid difficulties like these is to clarify, up front, exactly what it is that you do, and what you'll deliver.

For example, my proposal to clients always says, "Fees are for copy only." I make it clear that the copy is based on the background material supplied to me by the client, and that design, production, or other services are not included.

Never leave any room for doubt. Always confirm in advance with your client what the expectations are. Explain that if any additional work is required, then an additional charge will need to be negotiated.

What do you do when a client asks you to "write a slogan" during the course of a project? You have two choices. You can either say that you'd be delighted to *quote a fee* for slogan development. Or you could pass by saying, "Sorry, I don't handle slogans. But I'd be happy to refer another professional who does."

Warning Signs

Fortunately, most problems in your copywriting business can be avoided by watching for signs of trouble. When I started out, I was ignorant of the warnings listed below, and paid the price. Read this section carefully to avoid problems that will rob you of time and money.

BEWARE! Small agencies and design firms

There is nothing wrong with small ad agencies and design firms. Many can turn out to be excellent clients. But you do have to be careful. Small agencies and design firms, like any small businesses, are often run on a shoestring. They can be prone to bouts of cash flow crisis from time to time. I would be wary of any firm with fewer than seven full-time employees. I would be especially careful with solo operations (like mine).

How do you be careful? An easy way is to check the phone book or a business directory. If a client is listed, then he or she has likely been in business for at least a year.

Many copywriters I know routinely ask smaller clients to pay an upfront advance based on a percentage of the project estimate. If you ask for 35 percent, for example, and the project is quoted at $2,400, then you would receive a check for $840 before you begin work on the project. Advances are common in this industry. If a small client goes bust or can't or won't pay your invoice, you at least have some money for your work. If a client refuses to pay an advance, walk away.

You can also sleep better by getting a commercial credit report on a client, *before* you accept an assignment. A credit report provides you with information on a company's payment habits. Do they pay on time? How much do they owe suppliers? How long do they take to pay? Have they been taken to court for not paying an invoice? In the greater Toronto area, I can get a credit report on a company for $50. So, for larger value assignments, it's worth it to me.

A word of caution: If you suspect you'll have difficulty getting a client to pay your invoice, don't accept the assignment, no matter how lucrative and inviting it may be. It just isn't worth it.

BEWARE! Entrepreneurial startups

In your copywriting business, you're bound to receive calls from people just starting their businesses. These entrepreneurs will be full of enthusiasm for their businesses and will want you to be part of it. As a new venture, they are going to need a lot of collateral: a website, brochures, sales letters, sales proposals, ads — the works. They may also need marketing materials targeted at potential investors such as a CD-ROM presentation, corporate overview, or fact sheet. It's exciting and you're on the ground floor!

But be careful. New ventures can crumble to pieces just as quickly as they soar. Money is often an overwhelming issue — how to raise it, where to spend it, who is going to pay for what. An investor might pull out, leaving no money to pay vendors (like you).

You may be asked to work for a share in the venture. If you're a risk taker and you think this might be a good investment, consider the opportunity. But keep in mind it may be months, or even years, before you see any cash.

Many entrepreneurs begin a new venture with a less than clear understanding of their product and how it will fit into the marketplace. You may write a brochure targeted at sales managers, only to discover a week later that the best prospects are financial managers. You'll have to rewrite everything. Was this part of the quote? Will your client pay extra for the additional work?

My advice? Charge your full fee, plus a little more. Get a 30 percent to 50 percent advance up front. If the venture is serious and the players are dedicated and legitimate, they'll respect your professional approach and meet your terms.

BEWARE! New product launches

New product launches can be fun — and lucrative. A single new product can generate a multitude of projects: a PowerPoint presentation, packaging copy, a blurb for the website, a user guide, an alliance/channel piece, a direct-mail package.

You can obtain commercial credit information on companies in the United States at <www.Equifax.com> and in Canada at <www.Equifax.ca>.

"Do be wary of clients who promise loads of extra work if you agree to a low initial fee. There's a surprising number of amnesiacs out there."

— Diana Wimbs in her book *Freelance Copywriting.*

It's exciting being the first writer on a new product, but remember you're traveling down an unpaved road. There are no previous marketing materials that provide a neat summary of the features and benefits to cull from. You'll have to develop your key marketing messages from interviews, technical data sheets, white papers, memos, and other documents. Some of these will be well written and easy to follow. Others will not. Some will be accurate. Others, out of date.

If a client asks you to get involved with a new product launch, jump in with both feet. Just remember to quote sufficiently for the extra time involved.

BEWARE! Clients who want a cheap price in return for the promise of future work

You'll no doubt receive an offer from a client who says something like, "Hey Steve, we can't pay a lot for this assignment, but do a good job and there'll be plenty of work coming your way down the road." In fact, this happened to me just a few days ago. A very small ad agency asked me write a sales letter for them for half my normal fee. If I did, the agency assured me I would be the copywriter on any projects generated by the sales letter.

These are empty promises. Don't accept them. I have never experienced, or heard of a case, where a freelancer sacrificed his or her fee and was subsequently rewarded with a flood of new work. It just doesn't happen. What will likely happen is that halfway through the assignment you'll realize you've been duped — and you'll work in misery completing an assignment for only a portion of your normal fee.

Clients who offer me such deals are often surprised when I say no. I suspect these clients think all freelancers are struggling, and will chomp at the bit for such an opportunity. Even if times are tough, don't accept such an assignment. Trust me, the lure of "future work" is an illusion. It will never come.

To be diplomatic, when a client offers me such a deal, I reply with something like this, "This sounds like a great opportunity. But I make it a policy not to discount my rates on the speculation of future work. Perhaps we can negotiate a fee we can both live with?"

BEWARE! Assignments with no set deadline

A client gives you an assignment. You ask when the copy is due and she replies, "No hurry. Sometime within the next few weeks will be fine." Great, you think, I can complete this assignment at my leisure! No deadline pressures!

Wrong. Every assignment has a deadline. If you haven't been given the deadline, set one yourself. Why? Because if you don't, it's much too easy to put the assignment on the back burner. You'll whittle at it a little each day, but when a more pressing task surfaces, you'll set it aside. And then one day, your client will call and ask, "Hey, where's the copy?" And you won't have it completed.

When a client doesn't set a deadline for a project, I do. I ask the client, "Is three o'clock next Friday a good deadline for this?" Then I confirm the deadline — date and time — in writing.

BEWARE! Large approval committees

It's normal for your client to have your copy vetted by two or three colleagues in what is loosely termed in the industry an approval committee. This may include the marketing manager, technical manager, sales manager, art director, creative director, public relations manager, and others with a stake in the project.

An approval committee may not meet officially — no meetings in the conference room to chat about your copy — but your copy will make the rounds by e-mail, with each member freely inserting his or her comments. This is a normal process. In fact, it's common for you to receive two or three versions of your copy, each with separate, and sometimes contradictory, feedback. It's your job to consolidate the feedback, discuss with your client, and revise.

But what can happen when there are five, eight, or even ten people on an approval committee? Disaster. Many managers feel an overwhelming instinct to make comments and give opinions. I'm confident that if a page from *The Great Gatsby* was passed around a management team, there would be a flurry of requests for rewrites and corrections. If an approval committee has ten members, expect feedback times ten. And you will never satisfy them all.

If you are faced with your copy having to be approved by numerous people, be sure to take this into account when quoting the job. There are going to be rewrites, maybe lots of rewrites, so be prepared. Also, clarify the approval process with your client. Ask, "Who will have the final say?"

When you receive requests for revisions, go over them point by point with your client. Look for conflicting comments and be wary of vague, unclear feedback. Agree on which specific changes and revisions are to be made. Then get to it.

BEWARE! Handshake agreements

A few years ago, after sitting for an hour with a potential client discussing a project and agreeing to a price, I asked, "Can you give me a signed purchase order for this now?" He replied, "Actually, Steve, I work by handshakes only. If someone doesn't trust my handshake, then I don't want to work with them." Then he smiled and held out his hand.

He was actually trying to make me feel ashamed for asking for a signed authorization to proceed with the project! Unfortunately too many freelancers work on handshake agreements alone — until, one day, they get burned. Trouble is, you can't prove a handshake agreement. You can't take it to court if your client decides not to pay.

I get a signed authorization — confirming price and terms — on each and every assignment I handle, even from clients I trust and know well. I strongly suggest you do, too.

BEWARE! Signing confidentiality agreements that limit your ability to freely market your services

As a copywriter, you may find yourself working with sensitive or proprietary client information. Obviously, as a professional, you'll treat this information as securely as you would your own private business information. You would not, for example, fax details on your client's new product launch to his or her competitor!

Some clients, however, will want a stronger assurance that you won't mishandle their confidential information. This assurance often comes in the form of a confidentiality agreement.

Most such agreements are simple and straightforward. Others are arduous and filled with unintelligible legal jargon. Never sign a confidentiality agreement without reading — and understanding — it first. Beyond assuring confidentiality, you might find yourself signing away important rights.

One agreement I recently received from a client actually said I could not deal with any other company in their industry for the next seven years. This was a big industry. Did I really want to give up my rights to market to other companies in this industry in return for a $1,900 assignment? I asked the client to change the section to read "any direct competitor during the course of our business relationship." He agreed.

Another agreement I was recently asked to sign was from an advertising agency. It stated that any creative ideas I generated would belong to them — regardless of whether the ideas were applicable to the projects I would be working on for their agency or not. That one I refused to sign.

Make certain you understand every clause of any confidentiality agreement you are asked to sign. Never let a client rush you. Explain you'll need a few business days to review it. If you don't understand a particular clause, ask a lawyer for assistance. If paying for legal assistance isn't feasible, strike out and initial the suspect clause (which cancels the clause) and send it to your client. There is a good chance he or she will accept your change.

Of course, you should never accept work from a direct competitor of a current client, even if you haven't signed a confidentiality agreement. It's not ethical. As a copywriter, you become privy to competitive and sensitive product information that is not yet public knowledge. Obviously, your client will not want you to be in direct communication with his or her direct competitor — and you shouldn't be.

Being in the same industry, by the way, doesn't necessarily qualify as direct competition. I define direct competition as someone who offers a similar product or service, with the same benefits, to the same target market. Just because I write about life insurance for one company doesn't mean I can't also write about banking services for another company, even though both companies are in the financial services industry.

Also, once all the marketing pieces I write for a client become published, my confidentiality concerning those documents ends.

After all, everyone knows about them now. If there are no further projects to be had with the same client, I'm free to pursue other competing clients.

BEWARE! Disreputable marketers

You may be offered work by companies that are less than reputable. In some cases, you may find that their products or marketing tactics are unethical. In other cases, they may be downright illegal.

Fortunately, this doesn't happen to me that often, but I still get my share. For instance, I received a call last year from an immigration consultant who wanted a direct-mail package that looked like official government correspondence. I passed. Another company wanted me to write an e-mail promoting their website. Nothing wrong here, until I discovered they were going to blast that message to millions of unsuspecting recipients. (This is called spam.) Again, I politely said no.

Without doubt, you are going to write for clients that sell products that you wouldn't buy — or even endorse. But that doesn't mean you shouldn't work with them and write the most effective copy you can. After all, lawyers take on less-than-innocent clients all the time and doctors don't turn away patients because they don't like them.

But there's no reason to become involved in anything you think is unethical, immoral, illegal, or in any way contrary to your values. Trust me, it isn't worth the money.

12
Advice from the Pros: Three Famous Freelancers Tell Their Stories

Donna Baier Stein

Donna Baier Stein is a legend from a family of legends. Her father, Martin Baier, was a direct marketing pioneer in the insurance industry and is considered the father of Zip Code marketing. In 1989 he was inducted into the Direct Marketing Association Hall of Fame.

After earning a graduate degree in English, Donna worked as an administrative assistant for the Times Mirror Magazines, the home of *Popular Science, Outdoor Life,* and other magazines and book clubs.

When a position opened for a junior copywriter, she jumped at the chance. Four years and one relocation later, Donna decided to work freelance — eventually becoming one of the leading direct marketing copywriters of our time.

Donna is the author (with Floyd Kemske) of *Write On Target: The Direct Marketer's Copywriting Handbook*. It's considered a must-read industry standard.

How long have you been a self-employed copywriter?

"I started freelancing in 1980."

Why freelancing and not a corporate job?

"I love to write. I love to work alone. I wanted a variety of clients. I wanted to be my own boss and manage my own schedule."

How did you start?

"When I was a junior copywriter at Times Mirror, I had my own little office and a typewriter and I was thrilled. I wrote copy for their magazines and book clubs for three years and learned a lot about direct-mail copywriting. After Times Mirror I moved to Washington, DC, to marry my husband, and joined Guy Yolton's ad agency. I worked there one year."

Do you work mainly for agencies? Direct clients? Or a little of both?

"I work directly with some clients, and through agencies or other consultants with others."

Do you offer other services in addition to copywriting?

"I give seminars around the country for the Direct Marketing Association (DMA). One is called *Winning Direct Mail*. A second, on copywriting, will be launched this month through DMA. I speak at local direct marketing clubs and give writing and copywriting courses at universities and colleges. I work with several freelance direct-mail designers and can provide both copy and art to clients. I do not get into production or list management."

What, in your opinion, is the toughest business task for self-employed copywriters?

"Hard to say. I don't have trouble (generally!) working because I like to work and I like to write. After 20 years I'm generally pretty good about quoting appropriate rates. I learned the hard way to set deadlines far enough in advance to be fair to both me and to my clients. I have had some, though luckily few, difficult clients. The most difficult ones, I suppose, are the ones who have their own vision of what their direct-mail piece should be and don't want to listen to outside professional help. Another problem can be if a client gets feedback from x number of people and wants to include all their edits in the same letter. It's important that a letter sound as if it were written by one person, not by a committee."

How do you approach a new copywriting task? Do you have a defined process? Do you go by instinct?

"The first thing I do is read everything I can find on the product or service: back issues of a magazine, customer surveys, testimonials. I talk to the client and current customers, subscribers, and members. I fill my head with all the background information I can find. Then I let it sit a bit. Exercise is important to me in the writing process; it's often when I get some of my best ideas. I think it's important to fill your head with facts, then let the subconscious go to work.

"I start by writing out a list of 10 to 15 possible teasers for the outer envelope. I then start writing the letter. The first draft is always terrible. I go through numerous drafts and may find teaser copy in a late paragraph of my letter and pull it out. I work very hard on the response form to make sure the offer is stated the most succinct way possible. After I write everything I let it sit and tackle it again, taking out all kinds of unnecessary words — anything that's redundant or will slow the reader down. It usually takes me a good week to write a package."

What is your secret to success?

"I think I'm fortunate in being recognized as a top copywriter. I have a number of control mailings under my belt — packages I've written for clients that have not been beaten by other test packages. I have actively worked with both the Direct Marketing

Association of Washington and the New England Direct Marketing Association."

How do you promote your services?

"Most of my work at this point comes by word of mouth. I do have a website, <www.directcopy.com>."

What do you love most about being a freelance copywriter?

"I love to work with words. I love to write. I love to work alone."

What do you love least about being a freelance copywriter?

"Time crunches."

What advice would you give a freelance copywriter just starting out?

"Study the packages that are proven winners. Read the good books that are out there, by Bob Stone, Joan Throckmorton, and others. Read my dad's books [Martin Baier]: *Elements of Direct Marketing* and *How to Find and Cultivate Customers by Direct Marketing*. Work first for an ad agency or company to learn the ropes, *then* go out on your own. Do your best on every job you do and your portfolio will grow."

Bob Bly

Bob Bly is among the most accomplished self-employed copywriters in recent years. He is well known in business marketing circles, and has won several industry awards. He has also gained fame as a direct-mail specialist, receiving the prestigious Gold Echo Award from the Direct Marketing Association.

After graduating with a degree in chemical engineering, Bob held corporate positions as a technical writer and advertising manager before launching his freelance copywriting career. His success over the past 20 years is notable, especially considering he decided to try freelancing only after turning down a relocation request from his then employer.

Bob is a prolific author of more than 45 books, including several on copywriting, writing, direct marketing, and other business topics. His latest book is *Bob Bly's Guide to Freelance Writing Success*.

How long have you been a self-employed copywriter?

"Since February 1982."

Why did you decide to freelance?

"I don't have a natural tendency toward being a entrepreneur. In fact, I would have been happily employed the rest of my life in the corporate world except the company I was working for asked me to relocate to the Midwest. I would have gone, but my fiancée — who is now my wife — didn't want to go.

"In my job I was involved in marketing communications, so I thought maybe I could try doing this on a self-employed basis. I never knew any freelancers personally, but had met one or two through work. They seemed to be doing okay. So I thought I'd give it a try."

Why copywriting and not some other form of freelance writing?

"I never thought I could make a living writing books, because I never thought I could get them published. I hadn't written that many magazines articles, and had no idea how to make a living at that. I was working in corporate communications for Koch Engineering, so I was writing their brochures, and for my earlier job with Westinghouse I had done promotional videos and brochures. That's the kind of stuff I was writing, so I figured, why not start there?"

What struggles did you face early in your freelance career?

"Not just early in my career! I still have struggles to this day! Quoting fees is always difficult because every client is different and the market always changes. I'm doing this for 20 years and suddenly someone asks me how much I charge to write a website. A few years ago, I didn't have a clue. We just weren't talking websites when I started freelancing.

"Another problem I had is that I would go to meetings with people who expressed an interest in my services without really qualifying them, and I would waste a lot of my time.

"I also didn't know what to charge and usually didn't charge enough. Part way through my first year a client told me I should double my rates. I'm very conservative and I would always tend to underprice, which was a big mistake for many years."

Do you work mainly for agencies? Direct clients? Or a little of both?

"I don't have anything against agencies at all. But I work almost 100 percent directly with corporate clients. I have found there are fewer advantages and more disadvantages working with an agency, and more advantages and fewer disadvantages working directly with clients.

"In my particular specialty, which is direct marketing, the business is not controlled by agencies. It is a freelancer-oriented business. If someone wants a direct-mail package to pull subscribers for a $200 newsletter, they call a freelancer, not an agency."

What, in your opinion, is the toughest business task for self-employed copywriters?

"Number one, meeting deadlines and time demands. Not just the end deadlines, but the intermediate deadlines. For example, I might get a call from a client who says, "Bob, it's nine o'clock and we're all in the conference room. Can you talk for an hour?" And I really can't! Some people don't understand that.

"Number two is quoting the right fee. As I said earlier, it's always tough. And number three, dealing with the revision/approval process, especially in larger companies where it is done by a committee."

What is it that has made you so incredibly successful as a freelance copywriter? After all, you're a multimillionaire.

"It's two things. Plodding and longevity. If you just keep at it long enough, you reach a critical mass. I'm around in the market constantly. So I've just become known through the years.

"Another reason is focus. In the two areas in which I've specialized — direct marketing and business-to-business high-tech — that's all I did. So it's not that I'm smarter or a better copywriter than anyone else, I just got good at it through constant repetition.

"I'm also dedicated to study, to becoming an expert. For example, if another writer, who aspires to write TV commercials, had to write a brochure for a chemical plant, he or she might do it as an interim assignment, thinking it's boring or stupid. I, on the other hand, would really get into it. I would study the techniques, read other brochures, write articles, even read books about it."

What, in your opinion, is the best way to promote copywriting services?

"I won't say it's the best, but it was certainly the best for me, and that's the sales letter. I still think it's incredibly effective.

"Speaking engagements, when I accept them, are also very successful for me in two ways. First, if I speak at the right venue, I will always get an assignment from it, plus a lot of good leads. Second, preparing the speech is very educational. I have audio recorded many of my speeches and have used them as premiums for clients."

What do you love most about being a freelance copywriter?

"It's very simple. Writing. I love that actual act of writing. I could spend all day reading, writing, thinking."

What do you love least about being a freelance copywriter?

"I hate meetings, especially unnecessary meetings that waste time. I don't like the financial aspects of the business, such as doing taxes and keeping records."

What advice would you give a freelance copywriter just starting out?

"You should always study your specialty, and writing articles and books about it is a great way to do this. A new area for me is Internet direct mail. So what I did as soon as I got into it is I got a contract to write a book about it. So, of course, I know a lot about it because I studied it for six months, interviewed experts, and collected information. I always learn more when I write a book than the reader is likely to get out of it, although I hope the reader gets a lot out of it."

If you knew then what you know now ...

"I would have priced much more aggressively, earlier. And I would have learned to say no. I would have turned down many more things."

Any parting advice?

"One thing I learned that is very important. I got this from David Cohen, a freelancer in Florida. Live below your means. My income is well into the six figures, and I drive a ten-year-old Honda with 130,500 miles (210,000 kilometers) on it."

Ivan Levison

Ivan Levison is a testament to the power of niche marketing. Writing successful direct mail, e-mail, and websites, mostly for software marketers, he has achieved legendary status in that industry. Seth Godin, author of *Permission Marketing*, calls him "a true industry visionary."

Ivan worked as an English teacher for several years before joining a San Francisco-based advertising agency as a writer. He actually began his freelance copywriting career as a generalist before eventually making his name in high-tech.

Ivan is the author of the popular newsletter, *The Levison Letter*, which is published monthly by e-mail. (Subscribe at <www.Levison.com>.)

How long have you been a freelance copywriter?

"Twenty-one years."

Why did you decide to freelance?

"When I was working for an advertising agency in San Francisco, I started to do some moonlighting projects and pretty soon I started to see the potential. So I gave myself three months to jump out and see what I could do. As soon as I did, I could see it was a good fit for me. I realized pretty quickly that I could make more money than I could in an agency."

Why did you decide to niche your business in the software industry?

"When I started out, I was happy to do anything that I could. I wrote about food, financial services, high tech — the works. Then I began to feel that I was mile wide and an inch deep. I learned a little about a lot of things, but there was never any investment or deep knowledge of a particular area. Then, when I started to pick up a couple of high-tech accounts, I realized I could start to market myself just in this niche. When I marketed by niche — which was the software industry — things really took off for me."

Do you work mainly for agencies? Direct clients? Or a little of both?

"Only and unalterably with direct clients. I never work for agencies. Financially, I find it more advantageous to work directly with the client, because the agency wouldn't have to mark me up.

"Also, I prefer writing for the person who is paying the bill. They get to say what they need to say directly to me, without going through an intermediary. They have access to me. It's fast. They don't have to worry about shuffling the job through an account executive. It's better for both of us."

Do you offer other services in addition to copywriting?

"Copywriting is 90 percent of my work. The other 10 percent of my work is consultations by fax, phone, and e-mail."

How do you approach a new copywriting task? Do you have a defined process? Or do you go by instinct?

"I have a set of questions I have developed over the years that are in my head. I always start with a research session with a client and I review their materials, play devil's advocate, pull out the benefits, get them to sell me so I can sell the prospect. So I start with a solid research base. It doesn't have to be a long time. It could be an hour on the phone. Then off I go and write. I work hard and write and rework and write some more until I really like what I've got."

What is the one thing that has made you so successful?

"Putting all my effort into being well known in the software industry."

What, in your opinion, is the best way to market copywriting services?

"What has worked best for me is an integrated marketing approach. You go to the trade shows, you advertise in the publications, you talk at the conferences. I have clients say, 'Hey, I turn the page and there you are. I see you everywhere!' And it's all because of my little integrated marketing plan. And the best part is, anybody can do this, if you have a niche market. You can buy that top-of-mind awareness. I am a brand. I market myself as a brand. I pay money to have that brand recognized. I try to do everything in the marketing arsenal — the full spectrum — to market to my niche. And because it is a niche, I can. If I were just a generalist, I couldn't reach everybody. I can advertise in print, I can talk at conferences, I can attend trade shows, I can write columns, I can send newsletters ..."

What do you love most about being a freelance copywriter?

"Freedom — which is the ability to work with only nice people, people I feel congenial working with. Which, by the way, is easy in high-tech. They're a nice bunch of folks.

"I also enjoy the ability of any self-employed person to close up shop and take a vacation. I don't have to ask anybody for permission. I don't even mind getting the flu! I can take it easy and get well. In a salaried job I might get nervous that people are going to feel I'm slacking and so try to rush back.

"Of course, having some modicum of financial success is an important part of having this freedom."

What do you love least about being a freelance copywriter?

"It's the isolation of working from a home office, although I have a very nice one. I try to have lunch with friends, get out, but mostly I'm by myself. For a gregarious person it's relatively lonely. But I'm not whining. Most of my business I really love. So what if I have to eat by myself in a nice restaurant. People deal with tragedy all the time!"

If you knew then what you know now ...

"The biggest thing I learned in 21 years is that it pays to be a big fish in a small pond. Work the niche game, as I call it. For example, when I learn about a subject, when I learn about a new software product, it's not just thrown away because the next day I'm writing about wine. It's an investment in myself. In my future. Building a knowledge base. You build expertise, and that way you have something very valuable to offer clients.

Any parting advice to new freelancers?

"Pick a niche early. Don't waste years like I did. My career took off like a rocket when I picked a niche. It started when I went up to a software convention in Seattle. I went in and was working the room and people would say 'What do you do?' and I would say, 'I write marketing materials' and they would say 'Give me a call, here's my card, we really need some help in this area.' It didn't take me long to realize I was onto something!"

The following Checklists, Worksheets, and Resources are included on the CD-ROM for use on a Windows-based PC.

Checklists

- Is a Freelance Copywriting Business Right for Me?
- Copywriter's Office Set-Up
- Ideal Materials to Include in Your Book
- Marketing Package Checklist
- Other Materials You Can Include in Your Book
- Product Information Checklist

Worksheets

- Customer Information
- Fee Schedule
- Invoice
- Invoice Tracking
- Prospecting Tracking Form
- Product Master Sheet
- Product Questionnaire
- Project Planner
- Quotation Form
- Start-Up Budget

Resources

- Books
- Free Electronic Newsletters (e-zines)
- Course
- Audio/Visual Program
- Periodicals
- Associations